# Timesaver
# 40 Combined Skills Lessons
# for the Common
# European Framework

## (B1)

D1718766

Lynda Edwards

# CONTENTS

# INTRODUCTION

## What is the Common European Framework?

The Common European Framework (CEF) seeks to standardise the description and assessment of levels achieved in different languages across Europe.

**A1:** This is the first level described by the CEF and it refers to students in their first year or two of studying English. This can otherwise be referred to as Elementary.

**A2:** This is the second level which is usually reached by students who have been studying English for up to three years. This can otherwise be referred to as Pre-intermediate.

**B1:** This is the third level and describes students who have usually been studying English for up to four years. This can otherwise be referred to as Intermediate.

### 'Can-do' checklist

The Can-do checklist at the end of each unit tells the teacher and students what particular aspects of language the unit has practised. They are called 'can-do statements' as they concentrate on the language learners can successfully use in English, and are directly linked to the CEF descriptors for these levels. The contents page of this book indicates the topic and vocabulary areas covered.

## Why should I use this book?

This is the second book in the series and is a rich resource of lively, photocopiable materials for use with secondary-school students who have been studying English for up to four years.

This book is perfect for teachers looking for interesting skills work to complement a course book.

- The topics are fun and engaging for teenagers.
- Each unit is carefully staged to be both entertaining and achievable.
- Each unit presents and practises a wide range of new vocabulary.
- Each unit provides REAL language practice, linked to the CEF descriptors.
- Each unit provides practice in writing and speaking, and reading or listening.
- Each unit takes between 45-60 minutes of class time.
- Each unit provides a variety of activity types to give practice in all language areas.
- Each unit contains sufficient tasks to accommodate faster and more advanced students.
- Each unit has dynamic and engaging illustrations which will motivate students.

## How do I use this book?

 This shows that the unit is reading based.

 This shows that the unit is listening based.

The book is divided into several sections. Units 1–20 are suitable for students whose English is at the lower end of the B1 range and Units 21-40 for those whose English is at the higher end. Units 1–10 and 21–30 have a reading input and Units 11–20 and 31–40 have a listening input.

After each set of ten units there is either a reading test or a listening test which checks the students' reading and listening skills. The content of these tests is directly linked to the topics and task types used in the preceding units. The tests provide practice in a variety of task types that are currently used by national and international examination boards. After Units 20 and 40 there is also a vocabulary section which checks new items that the students have met in those sections of the book.

Within the sections, the units gradually become more difficult. (The grading of the units is a guide.) You may wish to use the more difficult units to stretch your students or easier units for less advanced classes.

The Teacher's Notes at the end of the book give ideas on how to stage the lessons. There are also keys to the exercises and transcripts for the listening tasks.

Select activities to give practice for language presented in your course book or simply for fun! Choose the appropriate units for your class from the contents page where you can find information about level, topic and language items practised.

Writing activities can be used for homework or done in class, at your discretion.

## Points to remember about teaching vocabulary and skills

### Vocabulary

- Students should extend their vocabulary as much as possible, as without vocabulary they cannot express meaning.
- Once vocabulary has been taught, make sure it is recycled and tested in various contexts for students to retain it.
- When explaining vocabulary give memorable examples – as many as you can. Students will remember an interesting or funny example much more than a simple explanation.
- Personalise your examples whenever you can. If a student feels involved, he/she will remember more easily.
- Encourage students to keep vocabulary notebooks. Encourage them to show you their notebooks on a regular basis.
- Remind students to always record new vocabulary in context so they can see both meaning and how the word works with other words.

### Speaking

- Encourage your students to speak as much English as possible at different stages of the lesson.
- Pair work and small group work allows for more speaking time for each student. It also means there is less individual domination and encourages shyer students to try more.
- It is better not to constantly correct as this can discourage some students from speaking and can interrupt the flow. If necessary, note down recurring mistakes for later work.
- Listen when the students speak and participate if you can, particularly while monitoring.
- Students will speak more if they are relaxed – so create a good atmosphere where they can laugh and have fun.

### Pronunciation

- Pronunciation practice is vital from an early stage even if it is simply "listen and repeat". Good pronunciation allows the students to be understood and also helps in developing their listening skills.
- Point out to students that pronunciation practice should not only focus on individual sounds. Linking and stress are also extremely important areas to practise.

### Reading

- Remind students that it is not always necessary to understand every word when they are reading.
- Give them practice in reading quickly to scan for information.
- Teach students how to deduce unfamiliar words from the context.
- Show students how they can often predict content from the title or other information.
- Encourage students to start looking at the differences between formal and informal language.
- Encourage students to read extensively for pleasure – magazines/books, etc. – and encourage them to speak about what they are reading in English.

### Listening

- Reassure students that listening as an isolated skill is rare. There is usually the opportunity for interaction or visual clues to aid understanding.
- Give students practice in using intonation clues.
- As with reading, remind students that it is not always necessary to understand every word.
- To improve listening skills the students should get as much practice as possible so that they can learn to distinguish words from the general "flow" of sound.

### Writing

- Encourage students to practise writing from the beginning. It is often the skill which is least enjoyed!
- Help them learn the difference between pronunciation and spelling.
- Writing allows consolidation of new language and therefore should be practised regularly.
- Writing is important for exams and future use of English.
- Give practice in writing for different purposes – e-mails, texts, applications, etc.
- Focus on the structure of a piece of writing, e.g. sentence linking and paragraphing.
- Give students time to discuss and plan their pieces of writing.

# 1 WHO WANTS MY...?

**1** **Tell your partner about:**

1 something you bought recently that you don't like.
2 something you bought recently that isn't the right size.
3 a present you received that you don't want.
4 something you have that you don't need anymore.

**2** **What do you do when you have something you don't want?**

1 throw it away ☐      2 give it to a friend or relative ☐
3 sell it ☐      4 exchange it ☐

Which of these is the same as "swap"? ..............................

**3** **There is a website called swaps.com where you can swap things you don't want for things other people don't want.**

What sort of things do you think people want to swap on this website? ...................................................................
..........................................................................................................................................................................

**4** **Here are some adverts from the site. Read them and match them to the pictures. Fill in the missing information on the pictures.**

**A** Would someone like to swap my old car for a bicycle?! I've moved to the city centre and I can't park my car here. It's a 20-year-old blue mini called "Milly". There are some holes in the doors and there is an unusual smell but she's a lovely car! Please contact me on ben@swaps.com

**B** My grandmother gave me a book for Christmas called "How to be Healthy". I really don't want it! Would someone like to swap it for another book or some CDs? It's a very useful book and it's brand new. It tells you what food to eat, what exercises are good for you, etc. Please contact pam@swaps.com

**C** Who wants to swap my designer dress for some other designer clothes? I bought a beautiful black Gucci dress when I was in Paris last month. Unfortunately it's too small and I've never worn it. I'd like some designer trousers (size 12) or a Dior handbag. Any takers? Contact rose@swaps.com

**D** Is anyone taking an English exam soon? I have an enormous English/English dictionary that I don't need anymore. It was very expensive – about £25! I passed my English exam (with its help!) and now I only use it to keep my door open! I'm going to be a nurse, so if anyone has anything useful – like a stethoscope – we can swap! Contact me at Becky@swaps.com

**E** I would like to swap an old collection of Elvis Presley CDs. This is a fantastic offer as they are probably very valuable now. I liked Elvis before but now I'd like to swap him for something modern, like The Scissor Sisters or Avril Lavigne. Anybody? Contact me at Tom@swaps.com

**F** Who would like my old laptop? It works well but I've got a new, fast one. It's a bit slow but it's a lovely colour – gold. It's quite heavy too but it's good for the muscles! Would anyone like to swap it for a new mobile phone with video? Contact pete@swaps.com

**5** Choose from the adverts A, B, C, D, E or F. In which advert does someone want to swap something that is ...?

| | | | |
|---|---|---|---|
| **1** unread | | **5** fashionable | |
| **2** big | | **6** heavy | |
| **3** outdated | | **7** unworn | |
| **4** tatty | | **8** a strange colour | |

**6** Read the adverts again. Then cover the texts and write the adjectives in the box with the correct nouns.

| Car | Book | Dress | Dictionary | CDs | Laptop |
|-----|------|-------|------------|-----|--------|
| | | | | | |
| | | | | | |
| | | | | | |

black blue
heavy fantastic
designer lovely
slow small
enormous brand new
valuable old

**7** Talk to your partner about these questions.

1 Which advert(s) do you think will be successful/unsuccessful?
2 Would you like any of these things?

**8** Speaking. Think of three things you would like to swap. Describe them to your partner and give your reason for swapping them.

**9** Writing. Choose one of your items and write the advert for the website. Who in your class would you swap with?

**Can-do checklist**

☐ **I can find and understand relevant information in an advertisement.**
☐ **I can give a straightforward description of an item.**
☐ **I can show interest and ask for information.**
☐ **I can write a description of an item.**

# 2 IT'S ILLEGAL

**1** **Use these clues to complete the computer puzzle and find the mystery word.**

**1** This is where you can talk to your friends online.

**2** You send or receive this from friends.

**3** Today this can be flat.

**4** You do this with your mouse.

**5** You need this to connect to the internet and you have to pay for it

**6** When you look at a lot of websites you do this.

**7** Write the mystery word here. _ _ _ _ _ _

What do you think this means?

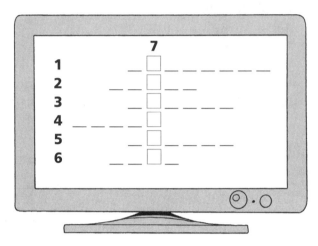

**2** **You are going to read a short article. Look at the title.**

**1** What do you think the article is going to be about?
a) a secret school
b) a new type of school

**2** What do you think happens at this school?

**3** **Read the text and answer the questions below. For each question circle the correct letter A, B or C.**

**1** Young people
A spend a long time at school.
B spend an hour a day on computers.
C spend a long time each day on computers.

**2** At "Hacker High School"
A they teach the children dangerous things.
B everything is a secret.
C teenagers learn useful things.

**3** The writer of the article
A thinks "Hacker High School" is a bad thing.
B is not sure if it's a good or bad thing.
C thinks "Hacker High School" is a good thing.

# HACKER HIGH SCHOOL

**"HACKING"** is the same as many other things that are illegal. It's interesting because it IS illegal. It's also dangerous, difficult and fun for young computer experts who spend more hours online than they do at school! So why is there now a "Hacker High School" in Spain? Why are they teaching teenagers the secrets of hacking? Isn't this dangerous?

The teachers at the school think that hacking is a serious problem. One reason is because it is a mystery. No one talks about it. At "Hacker High School" the students learn how to hack. There is no more mystery. The students practise hacking with phantom servers and they learn how to defend their computers. They also learn to be suspicious and to protect their machines.

When these students get better at hacking, will it make illegal hacking less enjoyable or will it make it easier?! It's an interesting and brave project. Will it be successful? What do you think? Send your comments to Computer News, Bartonby, Hampshire.

**4** **What do you think these words from the article mean? Choose A or B.**

1 illegal        A) against the law      B) very expensive
2 phantom        A) not important        B) not real
3 defend         A) build                B) stop something hurting you
4 suspicious     A) accept everything    B) think about possible problems

**5** **Talk to your partner about these questions.**

1 Do you think a Hacker High School is a good idea? Why/Why not?
2 Would you like to go to it? Why/why not?

**6** **Match these computer words with their meanings.**

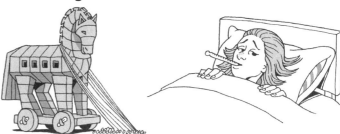

| | | | |
|---|---|---|---|
| 1 | VIRUS | a) | These e-mails ask for personal information. |
| 2 | FIREWALL | b) | This is something that looks OK but is really dangerous. |
| 3 | KEYLOGGING | c) | These are adverts and e-mails you don't want. |
| 4 | PHISHING | d) | This protects your computer. |
| 5 | SPYWARE | e) | This can kill your data. |
| 6 | SPAM | f) | This can follow your keys to get personal information. |
| 7 | TROJAN | g) | This secretly watches which sites you visit. |

**7** **Writing. With a partner write a questionnaire about using computers. Write full questions.**

**Using Computers**

1  How often ...?
2  Which websites ...?
3  Prefer e-mailing or phoning?
4  Send/receive many e-mails?
5  Chatrooms?
6  Server?
7  Safe?
8  A lot of spam?
9  Firewall?
10 Anti virus?

**8** **Speaking. Ask the other members of your class the questions and record their answers.**

**9** **Writing. Write a comment to "Computer News" about the article on Hacking High School.**

**Can-do checklist**

☐ **I can recognise significant points in an article.**
☐ **I can deduce unfamiliar words from context.**
☐ **I can write and use a questionnaire.**
☐ **I can ask for and give personal information.**
☐ **I can give a personal opinion.**

# 3 THE L♥VE OF YOUR LIFE

**1** **Unjumble the letters in these sentences to find words connected with dating.**

1 I met my girlfriend on a NILDB date.
2 I met my boyfriend at a TYRAP.
3 My aunt met her husband through a dating NYEGAC.
4 Some people meet their perfect partner through a SRALPONE ad.
5 I met my girlfriend LENION.
6 I met my boyfriend on DOYLIHA.
7 I met my girlfriend in a AFEC.

**2** **Talk to your partner about this question.**

Do you think people can find "true love" through agencies or advertisements? Why/Why not?

**3** **Read this notice quickly to find out what it is advertising.**

**4** **Find words in the notice which mean the same as**

1 stop and think ...................................
2 very important moment ...........................
3 most modern ...................................
4 ways of doing something .........................

**5** **Read the notice again. Cover it. How much can you remember?**

**Remember!**

Place: ...................................

Hotel: ...................................

Date: ...................................

Time: ...................................

Cost: ...................................

Contact: ...................................

## Who will be your perfect partner?

Would you like to know what sort of person will be your perfect partner? Forget all those magazine questionnaires! Come for a special PP (Perfect Partner!) analysis session with us. We will analyse your personality and tell you all about the future love of your life! We use the latest technology to look at how you react to different personality and physical types. We are giving an introductory talk on our techniques and a free first analysis in the Churchill Room at the Royal Hotel. It's on Tuesday 29th June from 7.30 pm until 10 pm. So don't hesitate! This may be the turning point of your life! Be prepared to answer lots of questions and you will leave with detailed information about the future Mr or Mrs You!

If you are interested phone
Julie Simms on 097862221.

**6** **Talk to your partner about these questions.**

    **1** Do you know what "Speed Dating" is?
       a) a very short date  b) meeting a lot of people for a very short time to see if you like them.

**7** **You are going to pretend to be a famous person at a speed dating session. On this card write down your information.**

> Name: ..............................................
> Age: .................................................
> Job: .................................................
> Interests: ..........................................
> Likes: ...............................................
> Dislikes: ...........................................
> Other information: ...........................
> .........................................................

**On this card write down some questions you would like to ask the other people at the Speed Dating Evening, e.g. *What is your favourite place for a holiday? What kind of pet would you like to own?***

> 1 ..........................................................
> 2 ..........................................................
> 3 ..........................................................
> 4 ..........................................................
> 5 ..........................................................

**8** **Speaking. Imagine your famous people are at a speed dating evening. You must find out as much information about the other people as quickly as you can. Use this information in your conversations. Remember you only have a few minutes for each conversation! Note down some comments for each person you meet.**

> Interesting?    yes!!
> Weird!    Good sense of humour!
> Strange!    Cool!    Funny!
> Nice clothes.    No!!    Boring!
> Brilliant!    Geek!    Brainbox!

**9** **Writing. Write an e-mail to a friend telling them about three people you met at the speed dating evening.**

---

**Can-do checklist**

- ☐ **I can find and understand relevant information in a notice.**
- ☐ **I can ask and answer questions about personal information.**
- ☐ **I can ask for and give detailed information.**
- ☐ **I can note down information.**
- ☐ **I can write a notice.**

# 4 JUST FOR LAUGHS

**1** **Match the words to the bubbles.**

A joke     A practical joke     A hoax

*"Have you heard the one about the man who went into a bar with a fish on his shoulder....?"*

*"Please telephone Mr. G. Raffe at the zoo for me.*
*"Hello. I'd like to speak to Mr. G. Raffe."*

*"Did you see the famous News programme in 1980 when they said that Big Ben (the famous London clock by the Houses of Parliament) was going digital and was going to have a new face? They said they were selling the numbers from the old face! The English people got really angry and there were lots and lots of complaints! Of course, it was April 1st!"*

**2** **Talk to your partner about these questions.**

1 What is special about April 1st in the UK?
2 Is it special in your country?
3 Can you remember any famous hoaxes on this day?
4 Can you remember jokes that people tell you?
5 Are you good at telling jokes?
6 Do you ever play practical jokes on people?

**3** **You are going to read some entries for a magazine competition to find the best practical joke. Read the entries and match them to the pictures.**

# COMPETITIONS

**A** *When I was at my first school we put some blue food dye in the fish tank to change the colour of the water. It worked and the water went bright green. Unfortunately it also killed the fish!*

**B** *When I was twelve my whole class played a practical joke on our teacher. We were in the new science room and it had new benches all round the room with cupboards under them. The cupboards weren't finished and they were empty. When the teacher left the room we crawled along inside the cupboards until all the students were hiding. There were 20 of us! We were very, very quiet. When the teacher came back her class had disappeared! She looked all over the school for us!*

**C** *My grandad wears false teeth and puts them in water every night to clean them. One day he used a new cleaner and was a bit worried that the cleaner was too strong. In the morning I emptied the water out of the glass and put a semi circle of pink toothpaste on the bottom of the glass and a semi circle of white toothpaste on top. I made some marks in the white toothpaste and put a little water over it. My grandad thought his false teeth had melted in the new cleaner!! It was very funny but he nearly had a heart attack and our mum got really angry!*

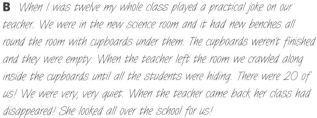

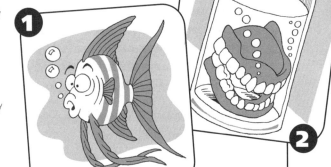

**4** **Find words in the texts that mean the same as:**

**1** not real .....................................

**2** move on hands and knees .....................................

**3** become liquid (often when it's hot) .....................................

**4** It changes the colour of things. .....................................

**5** **Which story ...**

**1** was nearly dangerous? ☐    **2** was about a lot of people? ☐    **3** had a bad result? ☐

**6** **Without looking at the texts, write the past forms of these verbs.**

**1** put .....................................   **6** go .....................................   **11** kill .....................................

**2** play .....................................   **7** have .....................................   **12** leave .....................................

**3** crawl .....................................   **8** come .....................................   **13** look .....................................

**4** use .....................................   **9** empty .....................................   **14** make .....................................

**5** think .....................................   **10** get .....................................   **15** be .....................................

Now test your partner.

**7** **Speaking. Can you tell your partner or the class a joke? Here are some expressions to help you.**

Have you heard the one about the ...?

There was this man and ... .

I heard this on TV.

Robert told me this.

I'm sorry, I don't get it!

That's really funny!

That's a good joke!

What's funny about that?

**8** **Writing. Look at these pictures and write the story of the practical joke for the magazine entry. Use this pattern:** One day ... .Then ... .When he ... . Suddenly he ... and he ... . He realised ... .

**Can-do checklist**

☐ **I can read and understand a story about an imaginary event.**

☐ **I can describe a real/imaginary event.**

☐ **I can write a description of an imaginary event.**

☐ **I can react to a story.**

☐ **I can link sentences and give a sequence of events.**

# 5 CHOCOLATE

**1** **Use the clues to make different words from the word:**

# CHOCOLATE

1  not early
2  not warm
3  wear on your head
4  a drink
5  you need this to build something

6  talk to a friend on the phone
7  a football trainer
8  you get this in a sauna
9  opposite of love
10  a short story

Can you find anymore?

**2** **How many adjectives can you think of connected with chocolate?**

..................................................................................................................................................................

..................................................................................................................................................................

**3** **Did you think of these?**

smooth  addictive
fattening  dark
sweet  messy
silky  milk
moreish  tempting
white  irresistible
sickly

Put the adjectives into the correct columns.

| Colour | Taste | Other |
|--------|-------|-------|
|        |       |       |
|        |       |       |
|        |       |       |
|        |       |       |

**4** **Look at these chocolate box lids. Match the names of the chocolates with the lids.**

*Dark, silky and smooth. Chocolates to tempt you. Chocolates to dream about.*

*Chocolates to die for! Once tasted ~ you're addicted for life!*

*Irresistable. Individual milk chocolates with a taste that is guaranteed to bring you back to this box again and again.*

| Chocolate of the night | More | Obsession |

**5** **Read this review and circle the correct letter A, B, C or D.**

**1** Why does the writer say "Danger. Danger. Danger."?
A Because these chocolates can make you ill.
B Because these chocolates are very expensive.
C Because these chocolates can make you fat.

**2** Why do you think the writer went back to the boxes so many times?
A Because it was really a difficult choice.
B Because the writer wanted to eat more chocolates.
C Because the writer had a lot of time.

■ **reviews** ■ ■ ■ ■

**Chocolate review**
Of the three new brands of chocolate on the market this week I can promise you the box to buy for that romantic date is "Chocolate of the night". It was a difficult decision. I had to go back to the three boxes many times before I could make a final choice! But, believe me – you will not be able to close the lid on this box! On a diet? Then be careful. Don't even look at it in the shop. Danger. Danger. Danger.

**6** **Here are some more addictions. Can you add any?**

coffee, cigarettes, sleep .........................................................................................................................................

**7** **Match these collocations.**

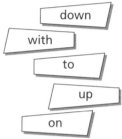

| | |
|---|---|
| addicted | down |
| hooked | with |
| give | to |
| cut | up |
| obsessed | on |

**8** **Speaking. Look at these expressions.**

*I eat too much chocolate.*
*I've tried that.*
*It's very difficult.*
*That doesn't work.*
*Any other ideas?*

*Why don't you ...?*
*You really should ... .*
*It would be a good idea to ... .*
*Have you tried –ing ...?*
*How about –ing ...?*

In pairs, choose an addiction and ask your partner for advice. Have the conversation.
Prepare your thoughts. Ask the rest of your class. Who gave the best advice?

**9** **Writing.**

Write a letter to a friend giving him/her some advice on giving up an addiction.

**Can-do checklist**
☐ **I can describe an item.**
☐ **I can write a description of an item.**
☐ **I can identify the writer's opinion.**
☐ **I can give my opinion.**
☐ **I can ask for and give advice.**

# 6 WORK OUT!

**1 Talk to a partner about these questions.**

1 What is a "Leisure Centre"?
2 What can you do at a Leisure Centre?
3 Do you often go to a leisure centre? Why/not?
4 What different jobs can people do at a Leisure Centre?

...........................................................................................

...........................................................................................

...........................................................................................

**2 Find twelve things you can do at a leisure centre in this wordsearch.**

**3 Quickly read this brochure about Southlands Leisure Centre to see how many of the above activities you can do there.**

```
A E R O B I C S K O
S Y O G A T I H I P
Q U E E T U R O C F
U S W I M P C P K O
A S T E I L U X B O
S A T E N N I S O T
H W E I G H T S X B
I N E A T O S T I A
B A D M I N T O N L
E D R I N K E N G L
```

## Try the new
## Southlands Leisure Centre

The new Southlands Leisure Centre has just opened its doors! You can find us at the end of Biggin Road and don't worry about parking because we have a huge car park. Buses stop immediately outside for those of you using public transport. We are an ultra modern centre with all the latest equipment and a whole range of facilities and classes for you to enjoy.

### Sauna
Relax in the heat of our sauna. Cleanse your body inside and out while you listen to soft music. Then jump into our snowpool to cool down. This is a wonderful sensation that will wake up your body and mind.

### Classes
We have many classes running throughout the day with our team of instructors. Kate, Niall, Gray and Frank can advise you which is best for you.
Classes include: aerobics, yoga, kick boxing, circuit training

### Pool
Get excellent exercise by swimming in our Olympic size pool. Sam runs swimming lessons for the very young and lifeguards Tom and Roberta are always there to keep you safe!

### The Gym
Our gym has the latest machines and equipment. Kate, Niall, Gray and Frank are also personal trainers and they can help you choose the right programmes.

### Courts
Ask Helen at reception to book a court. We have tennis courts, badminton courts, squash courts and five-a-side football courts. If you would like special coaching ask for Kev or Samantha.

### Cafeteria
Relaxing and exercise can make you hungry! Enjoy the healthy food and drink at our cafeteria. Here are some examples from the wonderful menu prepared by our chef Lionel.
Carrot juice
Rose tea
Mountain water
Cabbage burgers
Pea pizzas
Banana and mushroom pasta
Cucumber crisps
Curried apples
Garlic soup
Cauliflower casserole

### Creche
While you use the centre, leave your children in our Kids' Creche run by nursery nurse Jodie. There is also a play area for older children supervised by Paul and Jackie.

### Shop
Before you leave look round our shop and buy some beauty and exercise products to take home with you. Petrina is always there with help and advice.

**For more information about the Centre please contact our receptionist, Helen, on 06978 54463.**

**4** **Answer these questions.**

**1** Which road is the Centre in? .................................................................................................

**2** What can you listen to in the sauna? ...................................................................................

**3** How many types of court are there? ....................................................................................

**4** How many classes are mentioned in the brochure? ...........................................................

**5** Is the swimming pool big? ...................................................................................................

**6** How many personal trainers are there? ...............................................................................

**7** What sort of curry can you have in the cafeteria? ..............................................................

**5** **Read the brochure again and match these people with the pictures of their jobs.**

Jodie

Lionel

Sam

Petrina

Kev

Helen

Tom

Kate

**6** **Discuss these questions with a partner.**

**1** Which of these jobs would you like to do?

**2** Which of these jobs would you hate to do?

**7** **Speaking. Your college is taking a small group of students for a "career day" to Southlands Leisure Centre to see the different jobs people do there. In pairs decide how to spend the day so that you see a good range of interesting jobs. Include lunch and coffee breaks. Here are some expressions you can use.**

> We should start with ...
> Then we could ...
> After that I'd like to ...
> We could finish with a ...

> That's a good idea.
> How about watching ...
> Why don't we ...
> I don't really fancy seeing ...
> Let's follow ...

**8** **Writing. Write a plan for the day for your group.**

**Can-do checklist**

☐ **I can scan longer texts to gather information for a task.**

☐ **I can find and understand information in a brochure.**

☐ **I can make suggestions and plans.**

☐ **I can write a personal letter giving details of a plan.**

# 7 TELLING WHOPPERS!

**1** **These words all collocate with *tell*. Put them in order, 'best' to 'worst'.**

( a fib )  ( the truth )  ( a white lie )  ( a lie )  ( a whopper )

**2** **Talk to a partner about these questions.**

**1** Do you ever tell any of these?!
**2** Do you know when people are lying to you? How?
**3** Do other people know when you are not telling the truth?

**3** **Read this magazine article.**

Does it tell us  a) how to lie so that people don't know? ☐
                b) how to know if other people are lying? ☐
                c) how important it is to tell the truth? ☐

**4** **Read the article again and write the actions in the boxes.**

er...

## What a WHOPPER!

**Are you** a good liar? Are your friends? There are always times when we need to hide the complete truth but even with good actors there are ways to tell when people are lying and when they're being honest! Psychologists say that when we're not telling the truth we do certain things but we don't know we're doing them! You just need to look carefully for the signs to catch them out.

Look at the eyes. Are the speaker's eyes looking left and down? Or are the pupils getting bigger? It's a lie! A liar has to do something with their hands. So if the speaker is touching his ear or scratching his nose, be careful!

Another dead giveaway is blushing. Some people always go red. Also, liars smile a lot and talk quickly and loudly. Sometimes they even sweat a little and lick their lips or swallow because they're nervous. Other body language that can tell us if someone is lying can be crossing their arms or legs or tapping their toes.

Another sure sign is when someone hesitates or changes the subject. And be very careful. Girls are better at lying than boys!

**5** **Complete the collocations in these sentences with words from the article.**

**1** You can tell from her body ........................ that she doesn't really like him.

**2** Don't change the ........................ . It's important to talk about this.

**3** I know she's not keeping to her diet. There's a chocolate wrapper in her bag. It's a dead ........................ !

**4** I'm going shopping instead of going to school. I hope my mum doesn't ........................ me out and see me.

**5** We've got to keep our classroom neat and tidy this week. It's a ........................ sign we're

having an inspection!

**6** Test your partner. Do an action and your partner will tell you what you're doing. Or tell your partner to do an action and see if he/she does the right one.

Choose from these:

scratch your nose    sweat    swallow    tap your toes    look left and down

blush    lick your lips    cross your arms    hesitate    smile

**7** Use these clues to find the domino words. Each clue helps you find two words which end and begin with the same letter, e.g. tears?; that's true. = CR**Y**ES

**1** a small lie; you might go red

☐☐○☐☐☐☐

**2** you do this when you eat; a big lie

☐☐☐☐○☐☐☐☐☐

**3** get hot; move your feet

☐☐☐☐☐○☐☐

**4** no problem if you tell this; people can't find the words when they lie

☐☐☐☐☐○☐☐☐☐,☐☐☐

**5** these get big when you lie; you might do this to your nose if you are untruthful

☐☐☐☐☐☐○☐☐☐☐☐

**8** Speaking. Think of some questions to ask your partner about themselves and write them down, e.g. *Do you like Italian food? Did you do your homework last night?* Answer your partner's questions sometimes truthfully, sometimes not. Can you tell which are lies and which are the truth?

**9** Is it ever OK to lie? Talk about this using some of these expressions.

*I think …*
*I don't think …*
*What do you think?*
*It's no problem if …*
*It's fine if …*

*I agree …*
*I don't agree …*
*Don't you think …?*

**10** Writing. Write a short article for a magazine with the title:

Is it ever OK to lie?

**Can-do checklist**
☐ **I can find and understand significant points in an article.**
☐ **I can ask and answer questions about personal information.**
☐ **I can give my opinion.**
☐ **I can agree and disagree.**
☐ **I can write about my opinion in a simple text and give reasons.**

# 8 THAT'S THE LIMIT!

**1** **Find seven words in this wordsearch that go with 'limit'.**

Can you think of anymore? ..........................................

```
A S P E E D S
L M O W L A T
C O N E N M O
O N T I I D P
H E I G H T A
O Y R H T A G
L A E T I M E
```

**2** **Read these different pieces of information and match them to these limits. Where do you think this information can be found?**

**A** WE ARE SORRY BUT WE CANNOT SELL CIGARETTES TO ANYONE UNDER 16 YEARS OLD.

**B** You will be allowed up to 21kg of luggage. Extra will have to be paid for at check in.

**D** Only people taller than this mark can go on the Overunder Ride.

**C** ■ You have 1 ¹/₂ hours to complete this paper. Spend up to one hour on Section A and ¹/₂ hour on Section B.

**E** You can withdraw up to £300 a day. Please enter your PIN number now. ****

**F** In the UK the fastest you can drive on a motorway is 70mph. If you break the limit, you may have to pay a lot of money. Many of our readers think this is ridiculous. They would like the government to increase this to 80mph. Tell us your opinions.

**G** This Christmas remember! Don't drink and drive. It's easy to go over the limit and drink more than you're allowed and this can have terrible results. If you're going to drink – take a taxi!

**3** **Complete the sentences using *too* + adjective.**

**A** Sorry, you're .....................

**B** Sorry, it's .....................

**C** Sorry, you're .....................

**D** You're driving .....................

**4** **Correct the mistakes in these sentences.**

1 You can drive until 70mph in England.
2 Many people drink further than the limit at Christmas.
3 People beneath 16 can't buy cigarettes.
4 He crashed the speed limit and had to pay £100.

**5** **Here are some of the age limits in England. Complete the gaps with the numbers.**

1 You can leave school at .......... .
2 You can buy alcohol at .......... .
3 You can get married with your parents agreement at .......... .
4 You can get married without your parents' agreement at .......... .
5 You can buy fireworks at .......... .
6 You can drive a car at .......... .
7 You can ride a motorbike at .......... .
8 You can vote at .......... .
9 You can go to prison at .......... .
10 You can become a Member of Parliament at .......... .

In these sentences, what does can mean? a) ability  b) possibility

**6** **Talk to your partner about these questions.**

1 Are these age limits the same in your country?
2 What do you think about these limits?

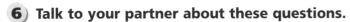

In my opinion...

I think...

That's ridiculous!

That's silly!

That's too young.

That's too old.

That's right.

I completely agree with you.

I completely disagree with you.

That's a good point.

No way!

**7** **Writing. With your partner think of some limits that there may be in the future. e.g.** *Children cannot own a mobile phone until they are 10.* **Use your imagination! Write a list of these limits.**

**Can-do checklist**
☐ **I can find and understand information in formal and informal notices.**
☐ **I can correct mistakes.**
☐ **I can use simple collocations.**
☐ **I can write imaginary notices.**
☐ **I can give my opinion, agree and disagree.**

# 9 PAGETURNERS

**1** **Talk to a partner about these questions.**

1 What do you think "pageturners" means?

2 How many kinds of books can you think of? Here are some anagrams to get you started.
**lerthilr   crenoam   videcette   rororh   if-ics**

3 Which do you prefer?

**2** **Look at the titles of two books and say what type of books you think they are.**

**A** Love in the Tropics

**B** Deadly Nightshade

**3** **Which of these words do you think you will find in the different books? Write them under the correct title.**

Love in the Tropics

..................................................
..................................................
..................................................
..................................................
..................................................
..................................................
..................................................
..................................................

| trees | swimming |
| lips | exciting |
| moonlight | blood |
| shock | pale |
| sunbed | relaxed |
| dirt | fixed |
| violent | prison |
| Gucci | dead |
| iced drink | handsome |
| heart | took off |

Deadly Nightshade

..................................................
..................................................
..................................................
..................................................
..................................................
..................................................
..................................................
..................................................

**4** **You are going to read the first paragraphs of each book. With a partner discuss what they will be about. Then use the words to complete them.**

### Chapter 1 **Deadly Nightshade**

The (1) ................ body was sitting under a tree. The eyes were open and (2) ................ , staring up at the night sky. The mouth was open too, perhaps in (3) ................ . No one ever thinks their death will be (4) ................ . The wet (5) ................ on her face shone in the (6) ................ . I knew the woman. It was Martha Tinsley, dead and in the (7) ................ behind her garden fence. It was Martha Tinsley with blood and (8) ................ on her (9) ................ face and on her long, white nightdress. It was Martha Tinsley, who would send me to (10) ......... .

### Chapter 1 **Love in the Tropics**

She was lying on a (1) ................ by the pool. Her long legs were tanned from the tropical sunshine and her fingers played with an (2) ................ on the table beside her. It was wonderfully hot. Gemma was (3) ................ , but a little bored and from behind her (4) ................ sunglasses she watched the (5) ................ young man dive into the water and swim strongly up and down the pool. Gemma smiled, her glossy (6) ................ showing perfect white teeth. Life was so (7) ................ ! Paul Tanner, the (8) ................ instructor, was half her age – but if he could make her (9) ................ beat faster? Gemma (10) ................ her sunglasses.

**5** Cover one text each. Ask each other these questions. How quickly can you answer?

**A** 1 Where was the blood?
2 What were her eyes looking at?
3 What was her name?
4 What colour was her nightdress?

**B** 1 Where was the sunbed?
2 Where was the drink?
3 What was her name?
4 What was the young man's job?

**6** Look at your text. Read it through and change some words. Read it to your partner. He/she must stop and correct you. Change roles.

> Did you say...?
> I'm sorry, could you say that again?
> I'm sorry, you've got that wrong!
> I think you mean...
> No! It's...!

**7** Look at these adjectives and put them into the correct columns.

boring   clever
exciting   scary
disappointing   romantic
funny   heavy
informative   terrifying
unputdownable
confusing

| positive | negative | either |
| --- | --- | --- |
|  |  |  |
|  |  |  |
|  |  |  |
|  |  |  |

With your partner can you think of the name or type of book to go with at least five of the adjectives?

**8** Speaking. Discuss these questions.

1 Do you like a happy ending? Why/not?
2 How do you think the two books from activity 4 might end?

**9** Writing. With your partner choose one of the books and write the last paragraph together.

THE END

**Can-do checklist**

☐ **I can read and understand a story.**
☐ **I can deduce the meanings of words from context.**
☐ **I can scan a text for detailed information.**
☐ **I can ask for repetition and confirmation.**
☐ **I can correct a person's mistake.**
☐ **I can write a story.**

# 10 THEME NIGHTS

### 1. Do this quiz with a partner.

1 Name three members of the royal family.
2 Name three famous English films.
3 Name three famous English books.

4 Name three famous English celebrities.
5 Name three English TV programmes.
6 Name three famous English pop bands.

### 2. Talk to your partner about these questions.

1 What do you think a "theme night" is?
2 Do you often go clubbing or to parties?
3 What is your favourite outfit for parties or clubbing?
4 Have you ever been to a "theme night" party?
   If yes, what was the theme and what did you wear?
5 What do you think would be a good "theme"?

### 3. Read the first paragraph of the e-mail below.

1 What was the "theme"?
2 Which famous Englishmen or women do you think were at the "theme night"?

### 4. Read the rest of the e-mail to find out which famous people were there. Choose from the list below.

**e-mail inbox**

Hi Jaz,

Why didn't you come to "Diva" last night? It was brilliant! They had an "English heroes and heroines" night and everyone dressed up as famous English men and women (mostly modern ones – not ancient people like Shakespeare!)

Tom came as James Bond. You can imagine! He looked really cool in his suit. And his younger brother came as Harry Potter. He only needed the glasses – he looks just like him! Lindy and her friends from Class J1 came as the Spice Girls. Lindy was the best as Baby Spice with a blonde wig and a mini dress. Your cousin, Mary, was The Queen of England – with a crown, obviously and the computer geek from Class J2 was wearing a long, multi coloured scarf and said he was Doctor Who. Have you heard of him? I haven't. Of course, Garth Needham came as David Beckham – who else!! He had all the right tattoos and hairstyle. There was also one strange old guy who was wearing a white flag with a red cross on it and said he was St. George! He was a laugh!

All night there was English music and we could buy English food and snacks(!!) It was a really good night and we got home very late. I'm SO tired today.

You must come to the next one.

See you at college,
Julie xxx

Prince Charles   The Queen   Sherlock Holmes   Harry Potter   Gandalf
James Bond   Agatha Christie   Elton John   Joss Stone   David Beckham
Posh Spice   Sporty Spice   Michael Owen   Tony Blair   Shakespeare

### 5. Write the name of the hero or heroine against these items.

1 scarf ...................................
2 glasses ...............................
3 mini dress ..........................

4 tattoos .....................................
5 crown .......................................
6 suit ..........................................

7 English flag ....................................

**6** Choose the correct answers, true (T) or false (F).

**1** Someone came as Shakespeare.   T/F
**2** Lindy has natural blonde hair.   T/F.
**3** Not everybody knows Doctor Who.   T/F.

**4** The Queen of England's name is Mary.   T/F
**5** Jaz and Julie work together.   T/F

**7** Speaking. You are going to a theme night and you have to dress up as Heroes and Heroines from your country. With a partner make a list of people who might be at the theme night and think of one item which would be important for each person to take (e.g. The Queen would have a crown, David Beckham would have a football).

Then, choose one character and tell the rest of the class which item he or she is taking.
Can they guess who you are thinking of?

**8** Writing. Write an e-mail to a friend about this theme night. Tell him/her how good it was, what you did and who came as whom.

**9** In pairs Student A looks at box A and Student B looks at box B. Ask your partner questions to complete the information in your boxes.

**A** James Bond was created by writer ................ and has become world famous because of the films. Many English actors have played James, including ................ Moore and Pierce Brosnan.

**B** Harry Potter is a famous schoolboy wizard created by writer J.K Rowling.

**C** The Spice Girls were a very popular girl band in the 1980s. They sang about "girl power". There was Posh Spice, Ginger Spice, Sporty Spice, Baby Spice and Scary Spice.

**D** Doctor Who is a Time Lord in a famous sci-fi series on British TV. There have been many different DrWhos since the 1960s.

**E** David Beckham is perhaps the most famous English ................ . He is married to Posh Spice (................ Beckham) and they have ................ children.

**A** James Bond was created by writer Ian Fleming and has become world famous because of the films. Many English actors have played James, including Roger Moore and Pierce Brosnan.

**B** Harry Potter is a famous schoolboy wizard created by writer J.K ................ .

**C** The Spice Girls were a very popular girl band in the ................ They sang about "girl power". There was Posh Spice, Ginger Spice, ................ Spice, Baby Spice and Scary Spice.

**D** Doctor Who is a ................ in a famous sci-fi series on British TV. There have been many different Dr Whos since the ................ .

**E** David Beckham is perhaps the most famous English footballer. He is married to Posh Spice (Victoria Beckham) and they have three children.

**Can-do checklist**
- [ ] **I can describe an event.**
- [ ] **I can scan text for detailed information.**
- [ ] **I can ask and answer questions about factual information.**
- [ ] **I can write a personal letter describing an event.**

# TEST 1 READING

## Part 1   Questions 1–5

Look at the text in each question. Circle the correct letter A, B or C.

**1** Where can you see this?

> **ANYONE OVER 12 YEARS OF AGE
> MUST PAY THE FULL ADULT FARE.**

A  college cafeteria
B  a train station
C  in a shop

**2** Where would you see this instruction?

> Please update your antivirus software.

A  in a doctor's waiting room
B  in a magazine
C  on your computer screen

**3** For what sport would you do this?

> *Talk to Katy at reception if you
> would like to hire a court.*

A  swimming
B  tennis
C  gym

**4** Where would you see this message?

> *Looking for new friends?
> Come along to room 7 at 8 p.m. on Tuesday
> for the first meeting of
> Totton College's Friendship club.*

A  on a noticeboard
B  in a newspaper
C  in a personal e-mail

**5** Where would you find this extract?

> Moreish and very fattening!
> But who cares?
> I tell you the taste is out of this world!

A  in a doctor's report
B  on a new box of chocolates
C  in a review of new food items.

## Part 2  Questions 6–10

These people want to buy something from adverts on the internet. Decide who will buy which items.

**6** Pete and Penny are getting engaged and Pete wants to get Penny something special for the occasion. She loves live music and the outdoors.

**7** Mary spends most of her free time watching television. She likes films and dramas. She is addicted to American soaps.

**8** Tricia does everything with her best mate Karen. They like clubbing and going out at the weekend with friends. It is Karen's birthday soon. Tricia wants to get her a present.

**9** Jane and Tom are married. They like travelling but they don't earn much money and spend most weekends walking in the countryside.

**10** Fiona and Greg have four children. They love watching classical music concerts on television but the rest of the family hate it so they listen to the radio instead.

**A** We're selling our fantastic tent and some camping stuff. It's in good condition and gives you everything you need when you're travelling. Of course it's not as comfortable as a hotel but it keeps you warm and dry and it's cheap! Only £50.

**B** Because of overspending at Christmas I unfortunately have to sell my favourite new Gucci handbag. It's pink, shiny and the real thing. For the girl who has taste and enough money it's a bargain at £45.

**C** I need to get some money to go on holiday so who wants to buy my complete *Friends* DVD collection? You can watch your favourite series as often as you want. £20.

**D** A bargain for anyone who wants to watch their favourite programmes in the peace and quiet of their bedroom. I'm selling my daughter's portable TV as she's leaving home. Only £50.

**E** My wife hates *Coldplay* which is unfortunate as we won two tickets to an open air concert next month. So, they're on sale for half price – £20 for the two. Any *Coldplay* fans out there?

## Part 3  Questions 11-20

Look at the sentences below about the first page of a romantic novel. Read the page to decide if the sentences are correct or incorrect.

If it is correct, circle A.

If it is incorrect, circle B.

| | | |
|---|---|---|
| **11** Mike's body was quite pale. | **A** | **B** |
| **12** Gemma stood up when he got out of the pool. | **A** | **B** |
| **13** Mike hasn't seen Gemma in the pool. | **A** | **B** |
| **14** Gemma thinks the water is cold. | **A** | **B** |
| **15** They were alone on the poolside. | **A** | **B** |
| **16** Mike thought Gemma was a good swimmer. | **A** | **B** |
| **17** She wore a swimming cap. | **A** | **B** |
| **18** Gemma swam up and down the pool once. | **A** | **B** |
| **19** Mike and Gemma know each other well. | **A** | **B** |
| **20** Gemma sat on a chair by the pool. | **A** | **B** |

Gemma was waiting for Mike when he stepped out of the pool. Water dripped from his tanned body. She handed him her towel.

"Is the water cold?" she asked, a smile on her lips and a sparkle in her eyes.

"Just perfect," he grinned. "Why don't you try it? I've never seen you in the pool."

Gemma dipped a toe in the water and shivered. "That's because I prefer iced water in my drinks."

"I'll get you one."

Gemma flashed him another smile and dived perfectly into the pool. Mike watched her in admiration as she swam up and down as smoothly as a fish. Other people at the poolside watched her too and when she stopped after ten lengths everyone clapped. She climbed out of the pool and shook her hair. Mike felt the drops of water on his hot shoulders. He was amazed. She had swum faster than he could but her breathing was still easy and calm.

"I didn't know you could swim like that," he said.

Gemma touched his cheek with her lips. "There's a lot you don't know about me," she whispered. Mike felt his face getting very warm. "I'll get us those drinks."

"That would be lovely," said Gemma as she lay back on the sunbed. "All that hard work has made me very thirsty."

## Part 4  Questions 21-30

Read the text below and choose the correct word for each space.

For each question circle the correct letter – A, B, C or D.

| | | | |
|---|---|---|---|
| **21** A event | B success | C perfect | D fun |
| **22** A clothes | B topic | C subject | D theme |
| **23** A in | B as | C for | D on |
| **24** A least | B all | C once | D many |
| **25** A who | B where | C what | D why |
| **26** A few | B one | C some | D none |
| **27** A job | B work | C cost | D minutes |
| **28** A at | B on | C in | D for |
| **29** A more | B over | C until | D many |
| **30** A wanted | B loved | C planned | D enjoyed |

# Southampton College Summer Party

The annual students' Summer Party at Southampton College on Saturday was a complete (21) ........ . The (22) ........ was Superheros and students came dressed (23) ........ every possible hero you can think of from Batman to David Beckham! I counted at (24) ........ ten Spidermen and there was also a President Bush. Not sure (25) ........ he was there! (26) ........ of the costumes were amazing and the students had obviously put a lot of (27) ........ into them. The food was excellent and all the music was from films. Very appropriate! The party began (28) ........ 8.30 and (29) ........ 200 people attended. Everyone (30) ........ the evening a great deal. Now the students have the long summer holidays to relax and wait for their exam results!

# 11 DAVID WHO?

**1** **Can you think of famous sports people whose names begin with these letters?**

B ........................................
E ........................................
C ........................................
K ........................................
H ........................................
A ........................................
M ........................................

QUIZ

1 Who is David Beckham?
...........................................
2 Who does he play for?
...........................................
3 Who did he play for in England?
...........................................
4 What's his wife's name?
...........................................
5 What is she famous for?
...........................................
6 How many children has he got?
...........................................
7 What are their names?
...........................................

Can you think of any more questions about David Beckham to ask your partner?

**2** **Do the quiz about David Beckham.**

**3** **There is a David Beckham Tour in South London where young David grew up. You are going to listen to the tour guide. First, complete the collocations with the words in the box.**

| pitch   pond   camp   goals   racing   box |

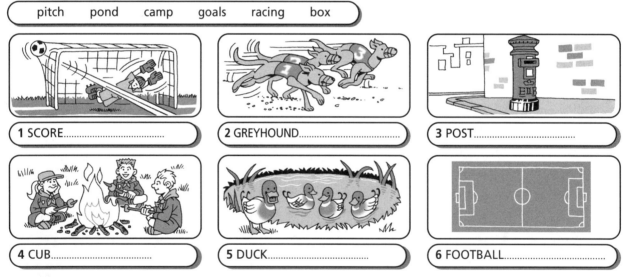

1 SCORE.............................

2 GREYHOUND.............................

3 POST.............................

4 CUB.............................

5 DUCK.............................

6 FOOTBALL.............................

**4** **Complete the directions with words from the box.**

| into   see   come   pass   on   on   along   past   see   on   see |

Go north (1) ............... Fullborne Road. You will soon (2) ............... the Peter May Sports Centre (3) ............... your right.

Turn right (4) ............... Chingford Mount Road. You will soon (5) ............... Walthamstow Stadium. Carry (6) ...............

along Chingford Mount Road. You will (7) ............... to Ainslie Wood. You will (8) ............... Chingford School (9)

............... your left. Carry on along this road until you (10) ............... a post box. Go (11) ............... a duck pond.

**5** 🎧 **Listen to the tour guide and match the places to the numbers on the map.**

Ainslie Wood ☐

Whipps Cross Hospital ☐

Chingford School ☐

Peter May Sports Centre ☐

Chase Lane Junior School ☐

Gilwell Park ☐

Larkswood Park ☐

Walthamstow Stadium ☐

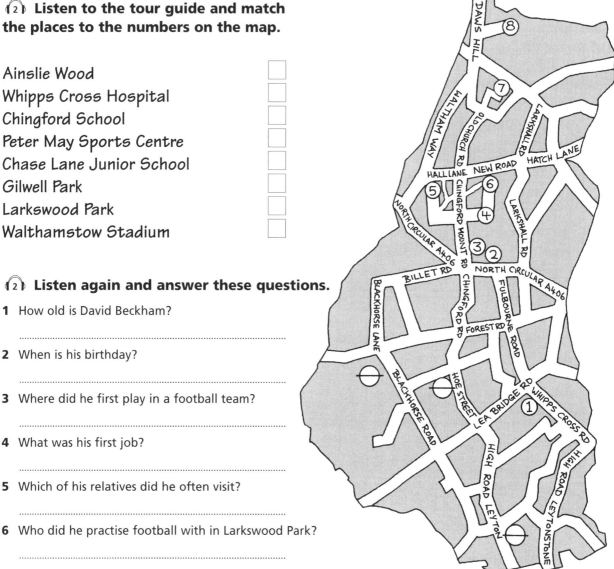

**6** 🎧 **Listen again and answer these questions.**

**1** How old is David Beckham?

.........................................................................................

**2** When is his birthday?

.........................................................................................

**3** Where did he first play in a football team?

.........................................................................................

**4** What was his first job?

.........................................................................................

**5** Which of his relatives did he often visit?

.........................................................................................

**6** Who did he practise football with in Larkswood Park?

.........................................................................................

**7** **Speaking. Add some more items to the map. Put them where you like. Choose your own or use these ideas, *a church, a hotel, a cinema, a shopping centre, a forest.***

Tell your partner where these places are without showing your map. Start at the same place as the tour guide and direct your partner to each place.

**8** **Writing. With your partner draw a simple map of your area. Imagine a childhood for a famous person and write the tour guide.**

**9** **Record this and let other pairs follow your map.**

**Can-do checklist**

☐ **I can identify specific details in a recording.**

☐ **I can understand detailed directions.**

☐ **I can give directions orally and in writing.**

☐ **I can write personal information about an imagined person.**

# 12 I WANT TO BE A MILLIONAIRE!

**1** **Talk to a partner about these questions.**

1 Do you like quizzes?

2 Do you think you have good general knowledge?

3 Do you like watching quiz shows on television? Why/not?

4 How many TV quiz shows can you name?

5 Which do you think is the best?

6 Would you like to go on a quiz show? Why/not?

7 Why do you think people go on quiz shows?

**2** **Complete these sentences with the correct answer A, B, C or D.**

**1** A person who takes part in a quiz show is a ...

| A member. | B competitor. |
| C quizzer. | D contestant. |

**2** Before an exam we often say that we are ...

| A frightened. | B nervous. |
| C forgetful. | D mistaken. |

**3** To get some money by answering questions correctly is to ... it.

| A earn | B take |
| C succeed | D win |

**4** To try to get a prize in a game is to play ... it.

| A for | B at |
| C on | D to |

**5** A word game is a ...

| A competition. | B race. |
| C puzzle. | D fight. |

**6** Something that helps you find an answer is a ...

| A note. | B guess. |
| C cheat. | D clue. |

**7** If you are stressed you should ...

| A relax. | B dream. |
| C lie. | D speak. |

**3** 🎧 **Listen to this conversation between a contestant and a presenter on a quiz show and complete the information below.**

**1** The contestant's name is ..................................... .

**2** He is from ..................................... .

**3** His wife's name is ..................................... .

**4** His children's names are ........................... and ........................... .

**5** He thinks £ ..................................... would be good to win.

**6** He would spend some money on a holiday to ........................... .

**7** He would also buy a ........................ for the bedroom.

**4** 🎧 **Listen again. Are these sentences true or false? If you think they are true, circle T. If you think they are false, circle F.**

**1** The top prize in the quiz is £1,000,000.   T   F

**2** Simon doesn't usually do quizzes.   T   F

**3** Simon's wife is at home with the children.   T   F

**4** Simon plans to buy two cars with the money he wins.   T   F

**5** **If you won £80,000, would you do the same things? Why/not?**

**6** In pairs, one student looks at the information for A and the other for B. These are the answers to some quiz questions. Write the questions with four multiple choice answers and then ask your partner.

**STUDENT A**

1 The capital city of Brazil is Buenos Aires.
2 The biggest ocean in the world is the Atlantic.
3 There are 8 bits in a byte.
4 The boiling point of water is 212 degrees Fahrenheit.
5 The language spoken in Brazil is Portuguese.
6 The highest waterfall in the world is the Angel Falls.

**STUDENT B**

1 The capital city of Iceland is Reykjavik.
2 The longest river in the world is The Nile.
3 Big Ben is a clock in London.
4 The two countries that border Uruguay are Brazil and Argentina.
5 The language spoken by the largest number of people in the world is Mandarin Chinese.
6 $H_2O$ is the chemical symbol for water.

**7** Look at these expressions the presenter said to help Simon calm down.

Is that comfortable?
How are you feeling at the moment?
Quite normal, Si.
Can I call you Si?

Just take some deep breaths.
Relax.
Don't worry.
It's going to be all right.

**Now listen and practise saying them.**

**8** Speaking. You are going to play another game with your partner. Student A asks Student B seven questions. Student B must not answer the questions until Student A has asked all seven questions. Then he/she must give the answers in the correct order. Change over. Use the expressions to help your partner to relax!

**STUDENT A**

1 What colour is the sky?
2 What's the name of the President of the USA?
3 What do we do when we're asleep?
4 What do the Italians eat with Bolognese sauce?
5 What can we see in the sky in the day?
6 What do we wear on our head?
7 What's the capital city of England?

**STUDENT B**

1 What colour is butter?
2 Which vegetable do the British often eat every day?
3 Where do you go if you are very ill?
4 What's the capital city of France?
5 Which animal gives us beef?
6 Who lives in a palace?
7 What is the name of our planet?

**9** Writing. Write your own quiz or puzzle for your partner. It can be one like you've seen in this lesson or it can be something else, *e.g. a crossword, hangman.*

**Can-do checklist**

☐ **I can ask and answer questions orally and in writing.**
☐ **I can respond to feelings of nervousness.**
☐ **I can ask for and give personal opinion.**
☐ **I can identify specific details from a recording.**

# 13 BEST MATES

**1** **Talk to a partner about these questions.**

**1** Do you think it's better to have
a) one best mate
b) a small group of really good mates or
c) a large group of good mates? Why?

**2** What makes a good mate?
**3** Do you think you are a good mate? Why/not?

**2** **When you are talking to mates, you use informal, colloquial language. There are some examples of this in the speech bubbles below. Match them to their meanings.**

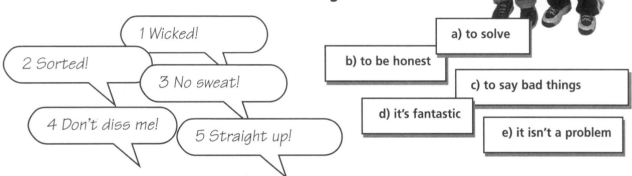

*1 Wicked!*

*2 Sorted!*

*3 No sweat!*

*4 Don't diss me!*

*5 Straight up!*

a) to solve

b) to be honest

c) to say bad things

d) it's fantastic

e) it isn't a problem

**3** **Listen to this radio phone in. Unjumble these sentences to find some questions about the phone in. Then answer the questions.**

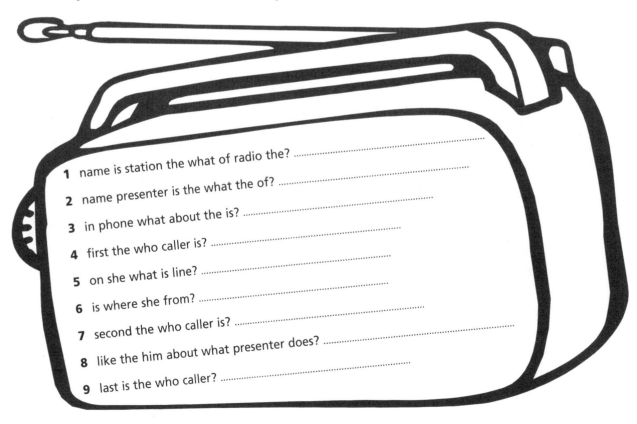

**1** name is station the what of radio the? .............................

**2** name presenter is the what the of? .............................

**3** in phone what about the is? .............................

**4** first the who caller is? .............................

**5** on she what is line? .............................

**6** is where she from? .............................

**7** second the who caller is? .............................

**8** like the him about what presenter does? .............................

**9** last is the who caller? .............................

**4** **Here are some more expressions we often use when we're speaking to friends. With your partner change the words in italics for the expressions in the box.**

> fancy    stuff    are into    clicked    hang out    left out

**1** When we first met we *got on very well*.
**2** We *really like* the same things.
**3** We like to *go out* together.
**4** We do *things* like go to the cinema together.

**5** We look after each other so no one's ever *on their own*.
**6** We usually *like* different sorts of boys!

**5** 🎧 **Listen to and practise these expressions of Pam's. The intonation is very important.**

"Duh!"          "I don't think so!"          "That is so true!"

**6** **Here are some more expressions we often use when we're speaking to friends.**

**Giving advice**

> *You've got to ....*
> *You shouldn't ever ....*
> *The most important thing is to ....*
> *Don't .... It's really important to ....*
> *You should ....*

**Showing agreement**

> *Right.*
> *I agree.*
> *I know what you mean.*
> *Yeah.*
> *Yep.*

**Now advise your partner on the problems below.**

**1** I really want to lose weight and go on a diet.
**2** I really want Jon/Kathy to ask me out.
**3** I really want to have a party at my house when my parents are away.

**7** **Writing. Write the advice for one of these problems as an answer from a problem page.**

**8** **Speaking. Work in a small group. Ask each other these questions.**

**Mates or Family?**

| | | |
|---|---|---|
| **1** Who do you talk to when you have a big problem? | Mates | Family |
| **2** Who do you like to go on holiday with? | Mates | Family |
| **3** Who do you buy better presents for? | Mates | Family |
| **4** Who is straight up with you more often? | Mates | Family |
| **5** Who would you prefer to share a room with? | Mates | Family |

---

**Can-do checklist**

☐ **I can ask for and give personal opinion.**
☐ **I can give advice orally and in writing.**
☐ **I can identify specific information in a recording.**
☐ **I can understand and use colloquialisms.**

# 14 YOU ARE FEELING SLEEPY

**1** Unjumble these letters to find a word connected with "sleep".

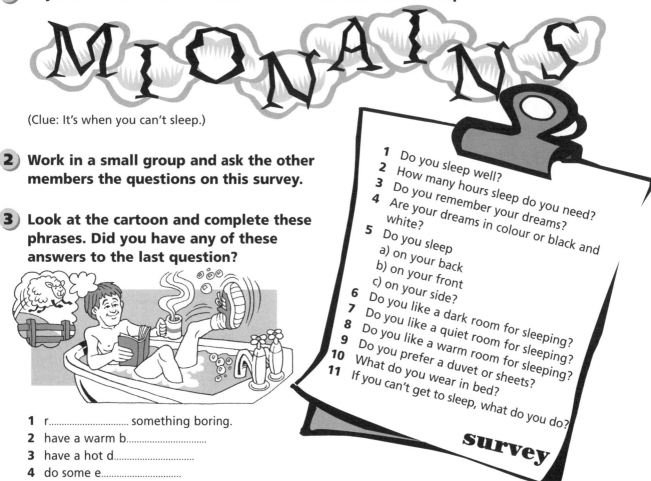

(Clue: It's when you can't sleep.)

**2** Work in a small group and ask the other members the questions on this survey.

**3** Look at the cartoon and complete these phrases. Did you have any of these answers to the last question?

1  r............................ something boring.
2  have a warm b.............................
3  have a hot d.............................
4  do some e.............................
5  count s.............................

**survey**

1  Do you sleep well?
2  How many hours sleep do you need?
3  Do you remember your dreams?
4  Are your dreams in colour or black and white?
5  Do you sleep
   a) on your back
   b) on your front
   c) on your side?
6  Do you like a dark room for sleeping?
7  Do you like a quiet room for sleeping?
8  Do you like a warm room for sleeping?
9  Do you prefer a duvet or sheets?
10 What do you wear in bed?
11 If you can't get to sleep, what do you do?

**4** These words are on the recording. Before you listen, circle the correct answers A, B or C.

1  What do we call a small area of water in a garden?
   A lake   B pond   C sea

2  What covers your whole body and goes brown in the sun?
   A dress   B hair   C skin

3  What is the opposite of "top"?
   A topless   B bottom   C down

4  If you put something heavy in water? It .....
   A sinks   B drowns   C falls

5  What do we call the main door to a house? The ..... door.
   A big   B front   C key

**5** You are going to listen to a sleep recording for people who have problems going to sleep. Before you listen, talk to a partner about these questions.

1  What do you think will be on the tape?
2  What will the voice be like?

**6** Now listen to the recording. Sit in your chair and follow the instructions.

**7** **With a partner, complete these sentences from the recording.**

1  Lie on your ...........................

2  Relax your ...........................

3  Close your ...........................

4  Breathe ........................... and ...........................

5  Your bed is like a ...........................

6  You are standing at the top of the ...........................

7  You can see down into the ...........................

8  Put your ........................... on the ........................... step.

9  The sun is shining on the ...........................

10  You're nearly at the ...........................

11  The lovely garden is ...........................

**⟨7⟩ Listen again and check.**

**8** **With your partner think of another situation like the house and the stairs and write notes for the recording instructions. Here are some suggestions.**

A  field – track – river – bridge – steps down – shining water

B  trees – path – light – clearing – pool – boat – beautiful woman

**Try to use some of these phrases from the recording:**

*I want you to imagine ....*
*You are in ....*
*You are standing ....*
*Breathe...relax ...walk ...move ...put ...*
*Can you see...?*
*Can you feel...?*

**9** **Speaking. Change partners and practise your situation on another student. Speak slowly. Does he/she go to sleep?!**

**10** **Speaking. Some people say that when you are in a very relaxed state like this you can learn and remember things very easily. When your partner is very relaxed say these things to him/her like the recording.**

**Student A**

A nap is a very short sleep. A nap. Nap.
To doze is to sleep very lightly. To doze. Doze.
A nightmare is a bad dream. A nightmare. Nightmare.

**Student B**

To snore is to make noises through your nose when you sleep. To snore. Snore.
A recurring dream is one that you have again and again. Recurring dream. Recurring.
To sleep lightly is to wake easily during the night. Sleep lightly. Lightly.

**Test him/her afterwards.**

**11** **Writing. Write the script you used in activity 9.**

**Can-do checklist**

☐ **I can understand spoken instructions.**
☐ **I can describe an imaginary situation.**
☐ **I can give instructions orally and in writing.**
☐ **I can ask and answer questions about personal information**

# 15 YOU'VE GOT MAIL

**1** **Talk to a partner about these questions.**

  **1** What sort of mail can you get?
  **2** Which do you use most?
  **3** Who do you usually leave voice mail for?
  **4** Some people hate leaving voice mails. How about you?

**2** 🎧 **You are going to listen to a person's voice mail. She has five messages. Listen and match the messages to these people.**

**3** **Here are some words and expressions from the listening. Choose the correct definition A or B.**

  **1** *grounded* means     A) not allowed to go out.     B) have to work in the garden.
  **2** *on behalf* of means     A) I represent     B) I'm the boss
  **3** *a fortnight* means     A) a month     B) two weeks
  **4** *a visitor's permit* means     A) special permission to visit     B) holiday parking
  **5** *assignment* means     A) an essay     B) an article
  **6** *on my own* means     A) in my house     B) alone

**4** 🎧 **Listen again and choose which message mentions these words.**

| | | 1 2 3 4 5 | | | | 1 2 3 4 5 |
|---|---|---|---|---|---|---|
| **A** | Costa del Sol | ① ② ③ ④ ⑤ | | **F** | free | ① ② ③ ④ ⑤ |
| **B** | midnight | ① ② ③ ④ ⑤ | | **G** | half an hour | ① ② ③ ④ ⑤ |
| **C** | offer | ① ② ③ ④ ⑤ | | **H** | attend | ① ② ③ ④ ⑤ |
| **D** | exercise time | ① ② ③ ④ ⑤ | | **I** | mate | ① ② ③ ④ ⑤ |
| **E** | friend | ① ② ③ ④ ⑤ | | **J** | promised | ① ② ③ ④ ⑤ |

**5** **Can you remember what conditions the callers gave? Write the full sentences.**

  **1** If you're not home/grounded ......................................................................................................

  **2** If you want to/visiting permit ......................................................................................................

  **3** If you do not attend classes immediately/leave the college ......................................................

  **4** If you send make fifty or more text messages a month/twenty extra ........................................

  **5** If you need a friend/be there ......................................................................................................

🎧 **Listen and check.**

**6** **Here are Angela's reactions when she heard the messages. Match them with the messages.**

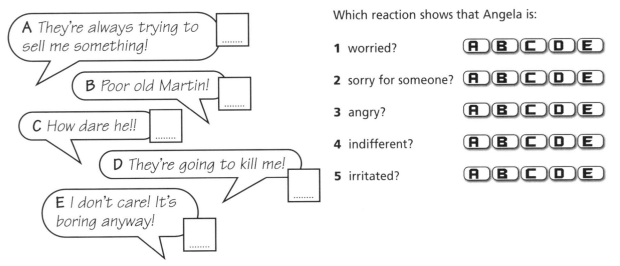

A *They're always trying to sell me something!* ........

B *Poor old Martin!*

C *How dare he!!* ........

D *They're going to kill me!* ........

E *I don't care! It's boring anyway!* ........

Which reaction shows that Angela is:

**1** worried?  A B C D E

**2** sorry for someone?  A B C D E

**3** angry?  A B C D E

**4** indifferent?  A B C D E

**5** irritated?  A B C D E

**7** **Listen to these expressions. Put them into the correct columns.**

| **1** | What a pity! |
| **2** | That's IT! |
| **3** | What shall we do? |
| **4** | Whatever. |
| **5** | He's a real pain! |
| **6** | So what? |
| **7** | Oh, no! |
| **8** | It's nothing to do with me. |
| **9** | Poor thing. |
| **10** | I'm getting fed up. |

| worried | feel sorry for | angry | indifferent | irritated |
|---|---|---|---|---|
|  |  |  |  |  |
|  |  |  |  |  |
|  |  |  |  |  |
|  |  |  |  |  |

**8** **Here are some expressions that you can use when returning a call. Practise saying them.**

*Thanks for your message. It was lovely to hear from you. Sorry to miss your call. I got your message.*

**9** **Speaking. Imagine you are Angela and your partner is the person who has left the message. You phone the person who has left the message. Have a short conversation. Change over and do the same activity with the next person who left a message.**

**10** **Writing. Write the reply Angela leaves to one of the people. Include one condition in your message.**

**Can-do checklist**

☐ **I can express surprise, irritation and other reactions.**
☐ **I can write a message.**
☐ **I can enter unprepared into conversation.**
☐ **I can use conditionals.**

# 16 THE BEST DAY OF YOUR LIFE?

**1** **Talk to a partner about these questions.**

**1** What has been the best day of your life up to now?
**2** Many people think that getting married will be the best day of their lives. Do you agree?
**3** Would you like to get married one day?
**4** If so, would you like to have a big or a small wedding?

**2** **Find twelve words connected to weddings in this wordsearch**

| | | | | | | | | | |
|---|---|---|---|---|---|---|---|---|---|
| C | D | A | L | B | E | S | T | U | B |
| H | M | N | P | R | I | E | S | T | U |
| U | O | H | A | I | R | S | T | I | T |
| R | O | R | O | D | R | E | S | S | T |
| C | N | S | P | E | E | C | H | T | O |
| H | G | U | E | S | T | A | R | G | N |
| G | R | O | O | M | G | K | I | I | H |
| R | O | F | S | A | L | E | N | F | O |
| N | A | V | E | I | L | P | G | T | L |
| T | U | V | I | D | E | O | I | S | E |

**3** Listen to four people talking about what went wrong on their wedding day and match the pictures with the speakers, 1, 2, 3 or 4.

**4** Listen again and tick how many of the words from the wordsearch you hear.

**5** **These words are from the recordings. Can you guess the meanings? Explain in your own words.**

**1** brilliant sunshine .......................................................

**2** stuck .......................................................

**3** reception .......................................................

**4** miming .......................................................

**6** **Circle the correct answer A, B or C?**

**1** In the first story
 **A** David lost the ring.
 **B** the bride put the ring on the wrong hand.
 **C** the ring was too big.

**2** In the first story
 **A** the guests had the reception without the happy couple.
 **B** the hotel delayed the reception.
 **C** everyone went to the hospital.

**3** In the second story
 **A** the bride and groom were ill on their honeymoon.
 **B** all the family were ill.
 **C** a lot of the guests were ill.

**4** In the third story
 **A** the bride went to buy a book.
 **B** the bride went to meet a popstar.
 **C** the bride didn't like the reception.

**5** In the fourth story
 **A** a pop video was made of the wedding.
 **B** a popstar made a video in a church.
 **C** the bride and groom sang a pop song together at the reception.

**7** **Match these different uses of *get* from the recordings with their meanings.**

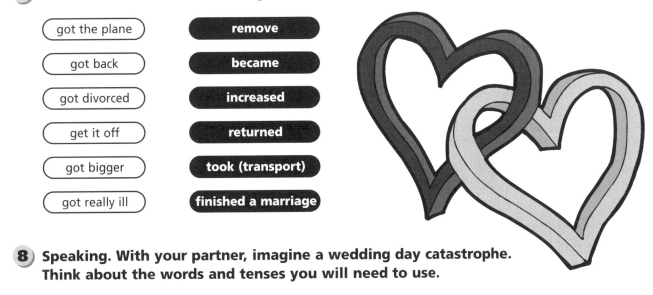

got the plane
got back
got divorced
get it off
got bigger
got really ill

remove
became
increased
returned
took (transport)
finished a marriage

**8** **Speaking. With your partner, imagine a wedding day catastrophe. Think about the words and tenses you will need to use.**

**9** **Writing. Write about this catastrophe in a short article for your local newspaper. Read your classmates' articles and decide whose wedding day catastrophe is the worst!**

**Can-do checklist**
 ☐ **I can understand short narratives.**
 ☐ **I can deduce meaning of unfamiliar words from context.**
 ☐ **I can describe an imaginary event.**
 ☐ **I can identify specific details of recorded material.**

# 17 JUST THE JOB

**1** **In groups, discuss these questions.**

**1** What sort of job would you like to have in the future?
**2** Do you think it's necessary to go to university or college to get a good job?
**3** What will be important for you when you choose a job?
**4** Would you like to have one job for your whole life?
**5** Is it good for students to have part-time jobs?

**2** **Use these clues to find the answers to the word puzzle. They are all things people think are important in a job. The mystery word is the name of a job.**

**1** I want several weeks .................................. each year.
**2** I don't want to work long .................................. .
**3** I want the chance to get .................................. ,
i.e. to get a better job.
**4** I want responsibility over other people and to
be a .................................. .
**5** I want a good salary with enough
.................................. to buy everything I want.
**6** I don't want difficult work. It
must be .................................. .
**7** I don't want to work outside but .................................. .

What do you know about this job? Answer these questions with a partner.

**1** What is this job?
**2** What other names are there for this job?
**3** Where does this person work?

**4** What sort of person do you think becomes one of these?
**5** What qualities do you think this person needs?

**3** 🎧(12) **Listen to two people, an older man and a young woman, talking about a door supervisor. Match the opinions of the speakers to the pictures.**

**4** **Which person thinks these things? Circle A for the old man or B for the young woman.**

Door supervisors...

**1** ... like fighting.  **A  B**

**2** ... are not friendly.  **A  B**

**3** ... earn good money.  **A  B**

**4** ... have a dangerous job.  **A  B**

**5** ... are not very clever.  **A  B**

**6** ... have to take tests.  **A  B**

**7** ... often have two jobs.  **A  B**

**8** ... do illegal things.  **A  B**

**5** Complete these sentences with words from the recording.

**1** He has no hair. He's .................................. .

**2** My sister's really short and thin. She's .................................. .

**3** He has a lot of friends. He's .................................. .

**4** She keeps calm and speaks to people in a polite way. She's .................................. .

**5** He's big with lots of muscles. He's .................................. .

**6** He works for himself. He's .................................. .

**7** She only works a few hours a day. She's .................................. .

**12** Listen again to check your answers.

**6** Speaking. Write questions to ask your partner about the jobs below. Think about: *money, holidays, promotion, easy/difficult, interesting, hours*

> hairdresser    politician    driving instructor    window cleaner    personal trainer

.................................................................................................................................................?

.................................................................................................................................................?

.................................................................................................................................................?

.................................................................................................................................................?

.................................................................................................................................................?

**Which of these jobs do you think is the most interesting?**

**7** Choose a job. Play 20 questions with your partner. He/she can ask you questions about the job but you can only answer "yes" or "no". You can ask up to 20 questions.

Follow this model:
Is it inside?
Do you need qualifications?
Do you have long holidays?

**8** Speaking. Imagine you are a career's officer at your college. Give a mini presentation for one of the jobs you have talked about.

**9** Writing. Write up your presentation. Begin:

To be a ... you need ...

**Can-do checklist**

☐ **I can understand factual information.**

☐ **I can write a straightforward description of a job.**

☐ **I can understand a speaker's opinion.**

☐ **I can give a short prepared presentation.**

# 18 NO ONE HERE BUT US ROBOTS

**1** How many words can you make from this word?

AUTOMATED

**2** **Talk to a partner about these questions.**

1 When you want to get information by telephone do you prefer to speak to a person or listen to an automated message? Why?
2 What automated information can we get on the phone today?
3 In what other jobs are people unnecessary today?
4 Do you think so much automation is good or bad? Why?

**3** 🎧13 **Listen to these short pieces of automated information and match them to the pictures.**

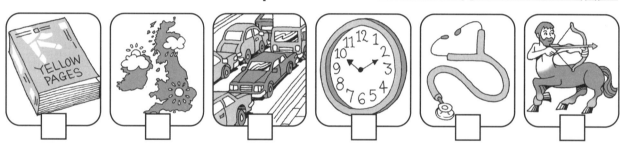

**4** **Would you phone any of these lines? Why/not?**

**5** 🎧14 **Listen to another automated message and decide if it is a serious recording or a fun recording. Give your reasons.**

**6** 🎧14 **Listen again. Choose the correct answers. Circle A, B or C.**

1 What is the name of the cinema chain?
  **A** Akon   **B** Ikon   **C** Ekon
2 Which town does the caller want?
  **A** Notting Hill   **B** Hampton   **C** Nottingham

3 How many films are on the list?
  **A** 5   **B** 6   **C** 7
4 How many showings are there every day?
  **A** 4   **B** 5   **C** 6

**7** 🎧14 **Listen again. The machine repeats the wrong information. What does it say?**

What is the correct information?

Film: .........................................
Date: .........................................
Time: .........................................
Tickets: ......

Film: .........................................
Date: .........................................
Time: .........................................
Tickets: ......

## 8 Which of these expressions did you hear on the recording?

Some of these expressions would be spoken by a real person, some by a machine and some by both. Show which by marking P, M or B for each expression.

| | | |  |  |  |
|---|---|---|---|---|---|
| 1 | ☐ | Let me finish! | P | M | B |
| 2 | ☐ | Please repeat. | P | M | B |
| 3 | ☐ | I apologise. | P | M | B |
| 4 | ☐ | Ah Ah! | P | M | B |
| 5 | ☐ | This is a bad line. | P | M | B |
| 6 | ☐ | Please speak clearly. | P | M | B |
| 7 | ☐ | I'm sorry I don't understand. | P | M | B |
| 8 | ☐ | Wait! | P | M | B |
| 9 | ☐ | Please speak up. | P | M | B |
| 10 | ☐ | Record your message after the tone. | P | M | B |
| 11 | ☐ | You have reached the … | P | M | B |
| 12 | ☐ | To change your message press "star". | P | M | B |

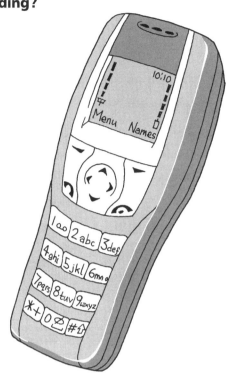

## 9 Speaking. Look at these different phoneline services. Choose one and say a few words the listener would hear when phoning the line. Your partner must guess which service. Change over and continue through the list. Try to guess from fewer and fewer words.

| | | |
|---|---|---|
| ✆ directory enquiries | ✆ news |
| ✆ horoscopes | ✆ speaking clock |
| ✆ health | ✆ dateline |
| ✆ weather | ✆ recipes |
| ✆ traffic | ✆ public transport |

## 10 Work in pairs - Student A and Student B. Dictate your numbers to a partner. Write down what your partner says.

**STUDENT A**
88930766522
77009336681
50999673449

**STUDENT B**
002E886h999
996L2lLEE00
2LS9888EEhh

## 11 Writing. With your partner invent and write a longer automated message. Record it and play it to the group.

### Can-do checklist
☐ **I can find out factual information.**
☐ **I can write a detailed message.**
☐ **I can ask for clarification and repetition.**
☐ **I can identify the general message in recorded material.**
☐ **I can use phone language.**

# 19 WHAT'S THE GOSS?

**1** In small groups, discuss the questions in the questionnaire.

**2** You are going to listen to some short phone conversations. Before you listen match the spoken words with their meanings.

| | |
|---|---|
| skinny | parents |
| hunky | to finish with |
| oldies | thin |
| an item | two weeks |
| to dump | to joke |
| to wind up | handsome |
| fortnight | a couple |

## Questionnaire

1 What do girls talk about when they're together?
2 What do boys talk about when they're together?
3 Do girls gossip more than boys?
4 Do older people gossip about the same things as younger people?
5 Do older people gossip more than younger people?
6 Do you gossip a lot? What about?
7 Why do people gossip?
8 What's the difference between gossip and chat?

**3** (15) Listen to these four short phone conversations and match each with the pictures, A–D.

**4** (15) Listen again and complete these expressions often used when gossiping!

**Starting a gossipy conversation**

1 You're never going to ................................. this!

2 ................................. who I saw!

3 Don't faint but did you ................................. that ...

4 What ................................. Becky Parks then!

5 Don't ................................. me you don't know!

6 Have you ................................. about ...

**Persuading someone to tell you something.**

7 Go ................................. . Tell me!

8 Come ................................. !

9 You know you're ................................. to tell me!

**Expressing surprise.**

10 You're having a .................................

11 You're .................................

12 You're ................................. me up!

13 N ................................. !

**5** In the last conversation, how does Jenny show disbelief?

**6** (15) Listen again and practise saying these expressions with the correct intonation.

**A:** They were in a stolen car.
**B:** A **stolen car**?
**A:** It was used in a bank robbery.
**B:** A **bank robbery**?
**A:** And there was blood in the car.
**B:** **Blood**?

**7** Work in groups of four. Each of you will read one of these sentences to your group. Each person will react to one part of the sentence.

Example:
**A:** I saw our headmaster roller skating with the maths teacher.
**B:** Our headmaster?
**C:** Roller skating?
**D:** The maths teacher?

1 Our football team is going to spend €20m on a new striker.
2 Sonja's father was on TV last night and he won €500,000.
3 My friend went to China for three days. She ate some snake.
4 We are getting an extra month's holiday because the science teacher accidentally blew up all the science labs.

**8** Speaking. Look at the statements below. With a partner have conversations about them. Take it in turns to start the conversation. Use as many of the above expressions as you can.

1 Your classmate's ex-boyfriend has gone to prison for stealing cars.
2 Your teacher has won a lot of money on the lottery.
3 Your classmate has a date with a pop star.
4 Your classmate got into a nightclub even though she is under age – she had a false ID.
5 Your sister used a fake tan and has gone orange.
6 Choose a subject yourself and surprise your partner!

**9** Writing. Change partners and have the conversations again but this time as in a chatroom. Choose who is going to start. Write the start of the conversation and pass the piece of paper to your partner. They write their response and give it back to you. Continue in this way. When you have completed your conversation, read it out aloud to your classmates.

**Can-do checklist**

☐ **I can initiate a conversation.**
☐ **I can express surprise.**
☐ **I can pass on information.**
☐ **I can ask and answer questions about personal opinions.**

# 20 DON'T SHOOT THE MESSENGER

**1** Talk to a partner about the questions on the fridge.

**2** 🎧 16 Listen to this phone conversation and make notes of what Terry wants Sue to tell Jackie.

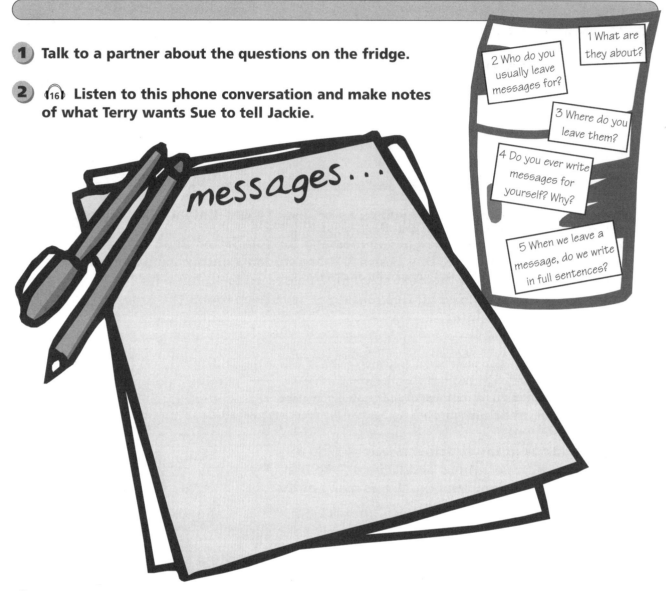

messages...

1 What are they about?

2 Who do you usually leave messages for?

3 Where do you leave them?

4 Do you ever write messages for yourself? Why?

5 When we leave a message, do we write in full sentences?

**3** 🎧 17 Listen to the second conversation and make any changes necessary to your notes.

**4** 🎧 18 Listen to the third conversation and make any changes necessary to your notes.

**5** 🎧 19 Listen to the final message and make any necessary changes to your notes.

**6** 🎧 16-19 Listen again to all the conversations and answer these questions.

1 Why can't they take Owen's car? Because ......................................................................................................................

2 Why does Jackie need to take the blue dress? Because ......................................................................................................

3 Why can't they go to the posh restaurant? Because ...........................................................................................................

4 Why can't they stay at the hotel for two nights? Because ..................................................................................................

5 Why can't they take Pete's car? Because ............................................................................................................................

6 Why is the posh meal on again? Because ............................................................................................................................

7 Why is it all off? Because ..............................................................................................................................................!

**7** **Here are some expressions Terry used to give messages and Susie used to take them. Write them in the correct speech bubbles.**

1 Tell her …
2 Do you want her to phone you back?
3 Could you tell her Terry called?
4 Can I give her a message?
5 Can you ask her to …
6 Right.
7 OK, go ahead.
8 Sorry about this.
9 Shoot.

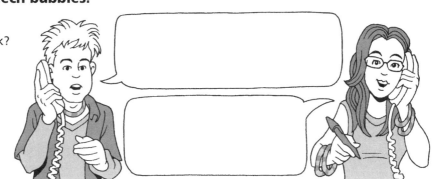

⌒20⌒ **Listen to these expressions and practise saying them.**

**8** **Speaking. You will be in a group of up to ten people in a circle - A B C D E F G H I J. Students A, C, E, G and I look at the message for your letter. Read the message to your partner – students B, D, F, H and J. These students must note down the message. Then pass it on (tell) to the next student (J passes on to A) but with TWO changes. Continue in this way until all five messages have been round the group. Then compare with the originals.**

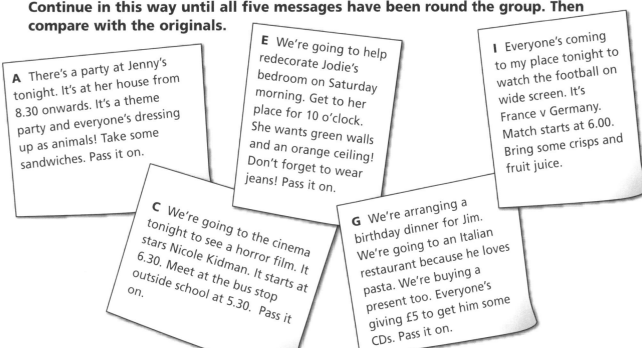

**A** There's a party at Jenny's tonight. It's at her house from 8.30 onwards. It's a theme party and everyone's dressing up as animals! Take some sandwiches. Pass it on.

**E** We're going to help redecorate Jodie's bedroom on Saturday morning. Get to her place for 10 o'clock. She wants green walls and an orange ceiling! Don't forget to wear jeans! Pass it on.

**I** Everyone's coming to my place tonight to watch the football on wide screen. It's France v Germany. Match starts at 6.00. Bring some crisps and fruit juice.

**C** We're going to the cinema tonight to see a horror film. It stars Nicole Kidman. It starts at 6.30. Meet at the bus stop outside school at 5.30. Pass it on.

**G** We're arranging a birthday dinner for Jim. We're going to an Italian restaurant because he loves pasta. We're buying a present too. Everyone's giving £5 to get him some CDs. Pass it on.

**9** **Writing. There have been phone calls for the following people. Write the messages.**

1 your mum or dad          3 your brother
2 your friend              4 your teacher

Begin each message like this: *Harry called….*

---

**Can-do checklist**

☐ **I can pass on factual information.**
☐ **I can understand messages.**
☐ **I can take notes.**
☐ **I can take and give a message.**
☐ **I can correct information.**

# VOCABULARY 1

**1** **Complete these sentences with the words in the box.**

1 My father and I tried to sort ................. the problem.

2 I'm always straight ................. with my friends.

3 I'm sorry but I don't agree ................. you.

4 In the quiz show they're playing ................. a holiday.

5 Did you throw ................. my old coat?

6 I drink about ten cups of coffee a day. I'm addicted ................. it!

7 Brian Forbes is married ................. my cousin.

8 My sister loves to wind my parents ................. .

| away |
| to |
| up |
| with |
| out |
| to |
| up |
| for |

**2** **Match these collocations.**

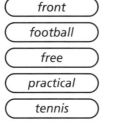

front          joke

football       lance

free           court

practical      pitch

tennis         door

**3** **Find and correct the mistakes in these sentences.**

1 My mother always taught me to tell a whopper.

2 I can nearly remember it. It's on the tip of my tooth.

3 The police stopped me because I passed the speed limit.

4 When he's hungry he often licks his nose.

5 I don't like leaving sound mail. I never know what to say.

6 I had an illness on my computer and I lost a lot of my work.

7 She phoned the company but only got an automatic message.

8 My friends met at a fast dating evening.

**4** **Replace the words in italics with a more informal word.**

1 Jack and Jill have been *a couple* for six months.

2 You must eat more. You're so *thin*.

3 Have you seen that *good looking* guy who lives next door?

4 Please take your *things* off the table.

5 He *finished* with her when he saw her with his best mate.

## 5 Underline the correct word in these sentences.

1 Try not to **hesitate/delay** when you speak English.
2 My brother always buys **designed/designer** clothes.
3 Her new film is very **hard/violent**.
4 His brother's clever on computers. He can **crash/hack** into any system.
5 We're going to spend a **fortday/fortnight** in New York.
6 Jen's parents **grounded/earthed** her because she was late home after the party.

## 6 Unjumble these letters to find the words.

1 ETRIPENCO .......................................... the party after a wedding
2 YED .......................................... change colour
3 WRACL .......................................... move on hands and knees
4 SCISSIUPUO .......................................... think something is wrong.
5 GLAILEL .......................................... against the law
6 FUTTOI .......................................... clothes
7 ITHEGH .......................................... how tall you are
8 MESSAGTINN .......................................... piece of work for school
9 LACTIMPODI .......................................... dealing with people politely
10 NANMOSII .......................................... can't sleep
11 SPOGIS .......................................... talk about other people
12 YNIT .......................................... very small
13 TELM .......................................... become liquid when it's hot
14 NIW .......................................... get the prize
15 DALB .......................................... no hair

## 7 Answer the clues to complete the crossword.

**Clues across**
1 You do this to send food and drink to your stomach
5 To protect yourself
8 You think about something all the time
12 Unwanted adverts on your PC
13 An exciting book or film
14 You go up and down these

**Clues down**
2 Not to tell the truth
3 I've had enough! I'm …. up!
4 The woman getting married
6 A small 1 down
7 How tall you are
9 What you look at on your computer
10 To exchange
11 How heavy you are

# TEST 2 LISTENING

## Part 1   Questions 1–6

There are seven questions in this part. For each question there are three pictures and a short recording. Choose the correct picture, A, B or C, and put a tick in the box below it.

**1** Where is the bookshop?

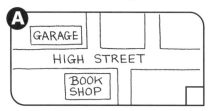  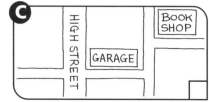

**2** Which of these puzzles does Pat prefer?

  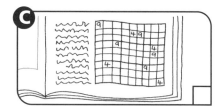

**3** Who does Tina go to with a problem?

**4** Where are you?

**5** What does Bill do?

**6** What happened at the wedding reception?

## Part 2    Questions 7–12

You will hear someone reviewing new programmes on television.
For each question put a tick in the correct box.

**7** John Parkes talks about TV programmes
A  every day.  ☐
B  every week.  ☐
C  every month.  ☐

**8** He liked
A  all three new programmes.  ☐
B  one new programme.  ☐
C  two new programmes.  ☐

**9** The quiz show contestants are
A  from two families.  ☐
B  from one family.  ☐
C  from a family business.  ☐

**10** The speaker thinks
A the questions are not easy.  ☐
B the questions are interesting for  ☐
   the people at home.
C the questions are easy.  ☐

**11** The wedding programme
A  uses films of people's weddings.  ☐
B  shows a lot of new things.  ☐
C  is very interesting.  ☐

**12** In the gossip show
A  famous people tell jokes.  ☐
B  famous people talk about newspaper stories.  ☐
C  famous people tell some stories.  ☐

## Part 3    Questions 13-21

You will hear a voice mail message. For each question fill in the missing information in the numbered spaces.

Message for (13) ...........................................................................

From (14) ...............................................................................................

He can't come to (15) ...............................................................

He has to (16) ...............................................................................

He's having dinner at (17) ...................................................

Later he's going to (18) ............................................................

He's staying at (19) ....................................................................

He's travelling by (20) ...............................................................

He'll phone again (21) ...............................................................

## Part 4    Questions 22–26

Look at the five sentences for this part. You will hear a conversation between a boy, Sam, and a girl, Debbie, about going to university. Decide if each sentence is correct or incorrect. If it's correct, put a tick in the box under A for YES. If it's incorrect, put a tick in the box under B for NO.

|  | YES | NO |
|---|---|---|
| **22** Sam thinks university is a good idea. | A ☐ | B ☐ |
| **23** Debbie is going to get bad marks in her exams. | A ☐ | B ☐ |
| **24** Debbie thinks money is very important. | A ☐ | B ☐ |
| **25** Sam wants the same things as Debbie. | A ☐ | B ☐ |
| **26** Debbie's parents know about her plans. | A ☐ | B ☐ |

# 21 WRITE ON!

**1** Complete this crossword using some of the adjectives from the list and find a word connected with handwriting.

1  You like being with people.
2  You like painting and music, etc.
3  You can do many different sorts of things.
4  You think good things will happen.
5  You get excited about ideas.
6  You like winning.
7  You never sit still.
8  You say what you think.
9  You have unusual ideas.
10 You are quiet with people you don't know.

| versatile | optimistic | competitive | artistic | outgoing | outspoken | lively |
| enthusiastic | | romantic | imaginative | shy | serious | funny |

**2** Discuss which of these adjectives your partner thinks describe him/her.

**3** Read this introduction to a new book about graphology and match the examples of handwriting to the words in the text.

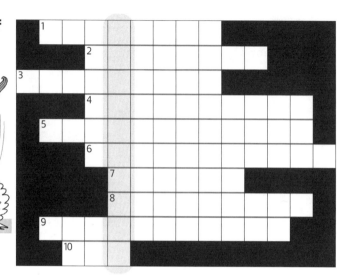

**Graphology**

What's your handwriting like? Is it large or small? Does it slant to the right, left or is it upright? Is it tidy or untidy? Are your letters rounded or thin? Do they have high upper strokes? Is the pressure heavy or light? Believe it or not your handwriting says a lot about you. Employers often ask graphologists to look at an applicant's handwriting to tell them some things about the person they might employ! Some people even ask graphologists to say if they think their personality matches their partner's before they get married!

**4** Which of these people sometimes ask the opinion of a graphologist?

**a)** a person applying for a job    **b)** a student    **c)** a couple    **d)** a boss    **e)** a teacher

**5** ▸ **Look at the pieces of writing. With your partner talk about what you think the writers are like. Use some of the adjectives from activity 1.**

**1** *Graphology helps employers find out about you!*
**2** *Graphology helps employers find out about you!*
**3** *Graphology helps employers find out about you!*

**6** ▸ **Now read the comments from the experts and match the pieces of handwriting to their descriptions. Were you right?**

**A** This writing is very neat. The letters are rounded which often means that the writer loves animals and children and is the sort of person who doesn't like arguing. The tidiness of the writing means that he or she doesn't like change very much, he/she likes to plan things and keep to the plans. The pressure is light and I think this person is quite sensitive and because the writing is in a straight line, he or she is probably quite a serious person. The upright letters can mean that he/she is also shy.

**B** This person is very strong, physically and mentally because there is heavy pressure. This also means that he or she is very outgoing, enthusiastic and optimistic. The letters slant to the right which shows that he/she is outspoken and lively and again the large writing means that this person likes other people to notice him/her!

**C** This person's handwriting has high upper strokes which shows that he is very imaginative and artistic. The letters slant to the left and the right and this means that he is versatile. The handwriting is large and bold which tells me that this person has a strong personality and likes attention. However, because his words are not always straight he often starts things but doesn't always finish!

**7** ▸ **Whose handwriting is it? Match the pictures to the comments.**

**8** ▸ **Talk about these questions.**

   **1** Do you think handwriting can tell us about a person? Why/not?
   **2** Do you write handwritten letters much or do you use the computer? Why/not?
   **3** Do you think we shall soon only use computers and texting for writing? Why/not?

**9** ▸ **Writing. Choose one of the questions from activity 8 and write a paragraph giving your opinion.**

**10** ▸ **Speaking. Swap your pieces of writing with your partner and look at the handwriting. Use what the experts said and tell your partner about his/her personality. Compare this with what you wrote down earlier about your partner. Is it the same?**

---

**Can-do checklist**

☐ **I can understand straightforward factual text.**
☐ **I can understand and describe descriptions of personality.**
☐ **I can ask for and give opinions.**
☐ **I can write a short essay.**

# 22 THE LATEST CRAZE

**1 What's a CRAZE?**

**a)** a silly activity    **b)** a popular activity    **c)** a confusing activity

**2 Here are two "crazes" from the past. With a partner see how many you can add to the list?**

1  Hoola hoops

2  Rubic cube

3  ...................................................................................................

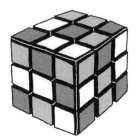

**Talk to a partner about these questions.**

1  What was a craze when you were a child?

2  What was your favourite craze?

**3 You are going to read an article about a craze. First match these words to the pictures.**

| time-consuming    addictive    maddening    rewarding |

**4 Read this magazine article about a new craze quickly to find why these numbers are important.**

1780        ...............................................................

1980s       ...............................................................

1984        ...............................................................

2004        ...............................................................

1,000,000   ...............................................................

10 years    ...............................................................

**5 Are these statements about the article true or false? Circle T or F.**

1  Sudoku is a type of crossword puzzle.        **T   F**

2  An Englishman invented it.                    **T   F**

3  There is a TV programme about it.             **T   F**

4  The world champion is British.                **T   F**

5  It's a game about numbers.                    **T   F**

6  It is very popular in England.                **T   F**

7  It was created ten years ago.                 **T   F**

8  It can take a long time to do.                **T   F**

9  You need to have good general knowledge.  **T   F**

## The Latest Craze ? ?? ?

Do you find crosswords difficult? Is your general knowledge not good enough for quizzes? Well, here's another way to spend a free hour or two! It comes from Japan, is addictive and people all over the UK are spending hour after hour trying to complete the numbers in these little boxes. It's maddening, time consuming but very rewarding! It's called *Sudoku* and you can buy books about it, play online and find one in every magazine and newspaper! You can even play on mobile phones and there is soon going to be a TV gameshow about it.

The very first idea for *Sudoku* came from a Swiss mathematician in 1780. It became popular in the USA in the 1980s and was then developed by a Japanese publisher in 1984. A main UK newspaper introduced it to the British people in 2004 and we can now find it everywhere!  The name in Japanese means "number single" and is so popular in Japan that over a million people play it every day! However, the winner of the latest online competition was British!.

*Sudoku* is popular because it is a game of logic and you can get better the more puzzles you do. But for how long will it be popular? Is it just a craze or will it still be with us in ten years' time? Who knows? Who cares?! It's great fun!

**6** **Read these instructions for the puzzle.**

**Instructions**

You have a box (grid) with nine rows and nine columns. There are nine 3X3 boxes inside the main box. These have a bold outline. Each smaller box must contain the digits 1-9. Each row and each column must also have the numbers 1-9. You must not repeat a number in a row, column or smaller box. Some numbers are in the box to help you. Easy puzzles have more numbers in. Look at this Sudoku puzzle.

Use these words to label each part: *row, column, grid, smaller box, digit, bold outline*

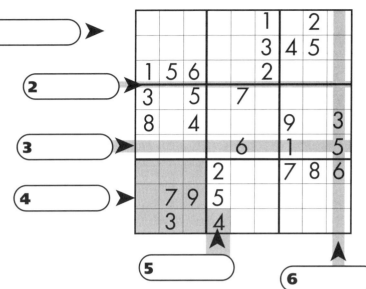

**7** **Here are some useful expressions you can use when you do a puzzle like this with someone.**

> *It could be 8.*
> *How about putting 1 here?*
> *Try putting 9 in that box.*

> *It can't be 3 because there's already a 3 over here.*
> *Let's look at this box.*
> *It must be 5.*

**8** **Speaking. Here are some popular puzzles. First match the names to the different puzzles. Then, with your partner talk about which you prefer and why.**

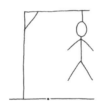

1. Who is David Beckham?
- - - - - - - - - - -
2. Who does he play for?
- - - - - - - - - - -

> Quiz      Wordsearch
> Crossword      Hangman      Anagrams

Here are some expressions you can use

saagnarm

> *I prefer ... to ...*
> *I like these better.*
> *I'd rather do...*
> *I much prefer...*

How often do you do puzzles like these?

**9** **Writing. With your partner choose one of these puzzle types and write your own to practise new words from this unit. Swap with another pair and try to do the puzzle.**

**Can-do checklist**

☐ **I can recognise significant points in an article.**
☐ **I can understand instructions.**
☐ **I can talk about preferences and deductions.**
☐ **I can talk about a past activity.**

# 23 THE FAT DUCK

**1** **Do you think "The Fat Duck" is the name of:**

**a)** a food magazine?   **b)** a restaurant?   **c)** a meal?   **d)** an animal at London zoo?

**2** **Read the first sentence of this article to see if you were right.**

**3** **Match these words with their meanings.**

1 good or bad opinion people have of something .................................

2 a sweet liquid .................................

3 a mixture .................................

4 they are on the tongue .................................

5 to make people want to do something .................................

6 the instructions for making a meal .................................

7 a verb usually used with "a bomb" .................................

**4** **Now read the rest of the article and answer the questions. Choose A, B or C.**

1 English food
A) is popular in every country.   B) has a bad reputation.
C) is delicious.

2 *The Fat Duck* is
A) very big.   B) very cheap.   C) very popular.

3 It is especially famous because of
A) its ice creams.   B) its mixed flavours.   C) its rare food.

4 Some meals at *The Fat Duck* have
A) helped teachers.   B) helped scientists.   C) helped chefs.

5 The writer thinks that a visit to *The Fat Duck*
A) will be exciting.   B) is for everyone.
C) is not a good idea.

**The results** of the latest search to find the best restaurant in the world are finally out! Today we can inform  our readers that for the first time the title goes to an English restaurant, *The Fat Duck* in Bray, Berkshire, owned by Heston Blumenthal.

This result may be a surprise to some of our foreign friends. English food does not have a good reputation. However, there is more to English cooking than fish and chips or boiled potatoes. A visit to *The Fat Duck* shows how imaginative English cooking can be!

If you can book a table at *The Fat Duck* (extremely difficult because it is so popular) you will find most unusual meals on the menu. This restaurant has become well known for its strange combinations of flavours. Would you like to try egg and bacon ice cream or fish sorbet? How about white chocolate and caviar, or oak and tobacco chocolates?

*The Fat Duck* is also famous for its unusual cooking methods. One excellent dessert from the menu uses nitrogen to freeze the outside of a type of syrup and when you put the frozen ball into your mouth it "explodes" on your tongue! Some teachers have focused on this scientific approach to cooking and taken some recipes into the science classroom. They think it is a good way to motivate their students. The students like the idea too!

A meal at the best restaurant in the world is not for everyone. It is certainly not cheap. You will need a couple of hundred pounds for two people. But, it is a very special place and a very special adventure for your taste buds.

**5** **Unjumble these words to find some questions about the text. Answer them.**

**1** Duck is The Fat what ?

**2** win it did title what?

**3** restaurant owns the who?

**4** it famous is why?

**5** dessert nitrogen why one use does?

**6** for meal a much does how cost two?

**6** **Read the beginning of the article again and match the words.**

( for )  ( known )  ( search )  ( results )  ( well )

( goes to )  ( title )  ( are out )  ( famous )  ( latest )

**7** **Can you remember the endings of these sentences?**

**1** The result may be a surprise to ...........................................................

**2** There is more to English cooking .................................................

**3** When you put the frozen ball into your mouth it ...........................

**4** They (teachers) think it is a good way .......................................

**5** It is a very special place and a very special ...............................

**8** **Talk to a partner about these questions.**

**1** What is your favourite restaurant?

**2** What is your favourite meal?

**3** Do you like any unusual combinations of flavours?

**4** Is there any food that you hated when you were a child but you like now?

**9** **Speaking. Here are some things that we think are important about a restaurant. Talk to each other about why these things are important and then decide which two you think are most important: *decoration, service, food variety, food quality, cost, comfort*. Here are some expressions to use.**

*Where shall we start?*
*What do you think about...?*
*I agree.*
*I think that's a good idea?*
*Which should we choose?*

**10** **Writing. With a partner design a menu for a new restaurant. Think of some meals with interesting combinations. Which restaurant in the class would win the "best restaurant" title?**

**Can-do checklist**

☐ **I can understand the main points of a newspaper article.**
☐ **I can scan text to find information.**
☐ **I can ask for and give personal information.**
☐ **I can use effective turn taking.**

# 24 MONEY IN YOUR POCKET

**1** **What is "pocket money"?**

a) money in your pocket at the end of the day
b) money for travelling
c) money that your parents give you

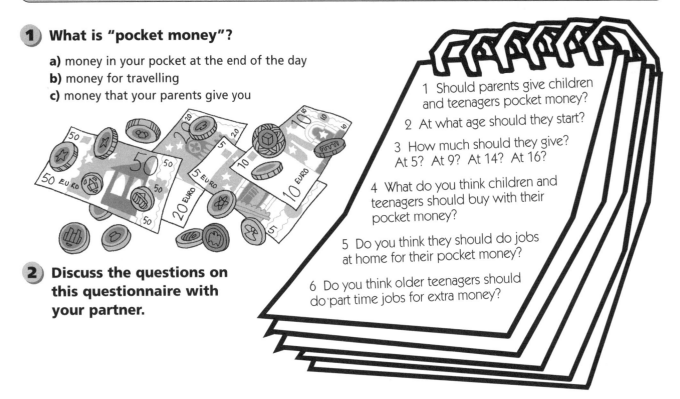

1 Should parents give children and teenagers pocket money?

2 At what age should they start?

3 How much should they give? At 5? At 9? At 14? At 16?

4 What do you think children and teenagers should buy with their pocket money?

5 Do you think they should do jobs at home for their pocket money?

6 Do you think older teenagers should do part time jobs for extra money?

**2** **Discuss the questions on this questionnaire with your partner.**

**3** **Read this chatroom conversation quickly to find the answers to these questions.**

**1** What's the name of Hayley and Jaz's friend?
**2** How much pocket money does she get?
**3** How old is Hayley's sister?
**4** What's the name of Jaz's brother?

Hayley: Hi there! How are things?

Jaz: OK. Do you want to go shopping tomorrow?

Hayley: Sorry. Can't. I'm broke.

Jaz: You don't have to spend much.

Hayley: But I can't even afford a coffee!

Jaz: You should get a part time job – like me. I work my socks off at the supermarket but it's good to earn some money.

Hayley: I'd love to but my parents won't let me!

Jaz: Then they should give you more pocket money!

Hayley: Yeah! Try telling them that!

Jaz: You know Carly? Guess how much she gets.

Hayley: A lot?

Jaz: She gets £190 a month!

Hayley: That's crazy! Her parents must be made of money!

Jaz: And her mum still buys her clothes and pays her hairdresser!

Hayley: Does she do any chores for that?

Jaz: She says she does jobs round the house. But I don't know, I think she's just spoilt.

Hayley: I think I'd like to be spoilt! My sister, who's 11, gets about £20 a month but with that she has to buy phone cards and sweets.

Jaz: My brother Tim is 8. If he keeps his room tidy he gets £2 a week for comics but he doesn't buy any and puts all his money aside! He's got loads now. He's probably saving up for his first car!

Hayley: Well, perhaps he can lend me some money to go shopping with you tomorrow!

**4** **Choose the correct answer A, B, C or D to complete these sentences. The words are all connected with money.**

**1** I usually spend €8 a week ................ sweets!
A in  B at  C on  D for

**2** We're saving ................ to go on holiday together.
A up  B on  C in  D for

**3** I ................ some money by helping my mum in the garden.
A do  B earn  C spend  D pay

**4** I can't ................ to go to the concert.
A afford  B make  C spend  D pay

**5** When I ................ some jobs around the house my parents give me some money.
A make  B help  C get  D do

**6** I haven't got any money this week. I'm ................ .
A empty  B spent  C broke  D finished

**7** When I'm older, I'll ................ some money aside each week.
A put  B save  C do  D get

**5** **Finish these sentences with words or expressions from the conversation.**

**1** A boring job in the house is a ........................ .

**2** To work as hard as you can is to ........................ .

**3** If your parents give you everything you want you are ........................ .

**4** Funny magazines for children are ........................ .

**6** **Pair these words together to make phrases.**

| | |
|---|---|
| SPEND MONEY | ASIDE |
| PUT MONEY | YOUR SOCKS OFF |
| SAVE | CHORES |
| CAN'T | ON |
| KEEP | TIDY |
| WORK | MONEY |
| DO | UP FOR |
| EARN | AFFORD |

**7** **Here are some expressions you can use when you give your opinion. Use them in activity 8.**

*I think they should ...*
*I don't think they should ...*
*I think/don't think it's a good idea to ...*
*I agree/don't agree with you.*
*What do you think about ...?*
*In my opinion ...*

**8** **Writing. Have a chatroom conversation with your partner. Use some of the expressions from activity 7. Do you think it's a good idea for students to have part time jobs? You can talk about:**

*studying, independence, getting too tired, value of money, what sort of job, learn about more than books*

You will need a piece of A4 paper. Student A begins the conversation and passes the piece of paper to Student B who responds and passes it back. Continue like this until the conversation is finished.

**Can-do checklist**
- ☐ **I can use a questionnaire to interview people.**
- ☐ **I can scan longer text to find information.**
- ☐ **I can ask for and give my opinion orally and in writing.**
- ☐ **I can understand simple collocations.**

# 25 THE BEAUTIFUL PEOPLE

**1** **How many words connected with physical appearance can you find in this word snake?**

**2** **Talk to a partner about these questions.**

1 Do you think it's important to look good? Why/not?

2 Do you think young people copy beautiful models and celebrities? Is this good?

3 There is a website called www.beautifulpeople.com. What do you think this website is for?
   **a)** selling beauty products   **b)** online dating   **c)** models

**3** **Read the first paragraph of this magazine article to check your answer.**

Only beautiful people can apply!
This is the message from a controversial new online dating website.

**4** **Read the rest of the article and do the task which follows it.**

Beautifulpeople.com is a website for the gorgeous to arrange to meet the gorgeous. If you are bald, have spots or big ears, don't even think about applying! Six of our journalists did – and only one was accepted! The others received replies which said, "We are sorry but our members do not think you meet our standards." So, what are the standards? How do you define "beautiful"? Here are the comments of Mark Banks who was accepted and Jenny Reilly who wasn't.

## Mark

I am not beautiful. I have a big nose and crooked teeth. My eyes are different colours and I have an ugly scar on my forehead. However, my mum thinks I'm beautiful and now, so I find, does this rather odd website! What a load of rubbish! I think it's very sad that so many people think that beauty is so important. And for so called "beautiful people" to only want to meet other "beautiful people" is, I think, simply stupid! This world is getting crazier and crazier.

## Jenny

My boyfriend thinks I'm beautiful and says that the people on the website are nuts! He says I've got lovely eyes and he adores my long, dark hair – but I think he's only saying that because he's my boyfriend and thinks that I'm upset about this silly website! But really – does it matter? It's who you are inside that's important not who you are outside. When people look at me I hope they're looking at the real me, not just the long, dark hair, big blue eyes, slim figure, perfect white teeth …Why did they refuse me? Why? Why? Why?!!!!!

**Here are pictures of Mark and Jenny. Without looking back at the article draw in the things they write about themselves.**

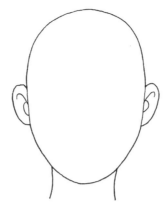

**5** **Read these statements about the article and choose true (T) or false (F).**

1 Beautifulpeople.com is for everyone.                                    **T   F**
2 New people are chosen by members of the website.        **T   F**
3 Some people think it's a good idea and some think it's a bad idea.   **T   F**
4 Mark is happy that he was accepted.                           **T   F**
5 Jenny says she likes people to think she's beautiful.       **T   F**
6 Jenny's boyfriend thinks she's upset.                         **T   F**

**6** **Here are some verbs from the article. Write the nouns from them.**

**1** define  ................................................
**2** arrange  ................................................
**3** apply  ................................................

**4** accept  ................................................
**5** refuse  ................................................
**6** adore  ................................................

**7** **Mark says that the world is getting crazier and crazier. With your partner think of things that are getting:**

| more and more difficult | more and more expensive | longer and longer | bigger and bigger | noisier and noisier |

**8** **Speaking. Talk to a partner about these questions.**

1 Do you think it's important to be beautiful?
2 Do you think beautiful people get better jobs?
3 Do you think beautiful people usually have beautiful partners?
4 Do you think beautiful people have better lives?

**9** **Writing. With your partner choose five famous beautiful people to apply to join the website. Choose men and women. Write a short description for the website. Start:**

*My name is Nicole Kidman and I'm a beautiful person.*

**Can-do checklist**

☐ **I can write a physical description.**
☐ **I can talk about change.**
☐ **I can ask for and give opinion.**
☐ **I can make nouns from verbs.**

# 26 I'M HAVING A BAD DAY

**1** Use these clues to complete the crossword and find the mystery word. The words are all connected with exams!

1 To work very hard at the last minute.
2 A small exam.
3 How you feel before an exam.
4 To take an exam again.
5 What you suffer from when lots of things go wrong.
6 Not to pass the exam.
7 Not to remember.
8 There are many of these in your exam paper.

Mystery word: .......................

**2** Sometimes you can have a "good day" or a "bad day" when you take an exam or a test. With your partner think of some things that can make you have a "bad day".

**3** You are going to read an e-mail from an English penfriend. Read it quickly to identify the main subject of the letter. Choose A, B or C.

**A)** exam questions    **B)** exam marks    **C)** exam tips

## e-mail inbox

Hi Lisa!
Are you OK? I'm a bit fed up. We've got exams next week so I'm working hard. I get so nervous before exams and I forget everything! I never do very well. How about you?
I must tell you – there's this new thing in exams in England. They say that if you have a lot of stress on your exam day (not just because of the exam!!) you can get extra marks! Isn't that cool?! Can you believe it? If you have a bad cold, it's an extra 2% and for a headache it's 1%. If your pet dies on the morning of the exam, you get 2% more or if it dies the day before, you get 1%. If someone in your family is ill, you get extra too – even if it's a distant cousin! Up to 4%!!
There's this really funny website called www.examexcuse.com where people write funny excuses to get extra marks! Have a look! I'm attaching one of the excuses!
Well – I'm fine, my family's fine (including my distant cousins!) and the pet's fine so I'd better do some work!
Bye!
Lynne xxxx

### 4 Read the e-mail again and choose the correct answer A, B or C.

1 **A)** Lynne loves exams.   **B)** Lynne is usually good at exams.   **C)** Lynne can't remember things in exams.

2 **A)** You can get extra marks if your cousin is ill.   **B)** You can get extra marks if you know the examiner.
**C)** You lose marks if you are late.

3 **A)** The website is for jokes about exams.   **B)** The website is for serious exam advice.   **C)** The website
gives excuses for doing a bad exam.

4 **A)** Lynne can't get extra marks.   **B)** Lynne's pet is ill.   **C)** Lynne hasn't done any work.

### 5 Read the excuse on the website and put the pictures in order to show the story. How many extra points will the writer get?

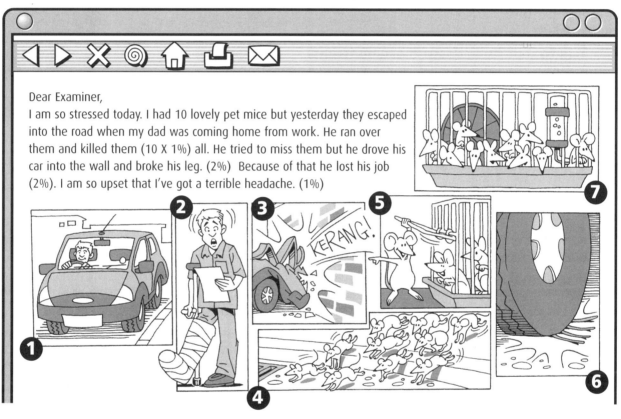

Dear Examiner,
I am so stressed today. I had 10 lovely pet mice but yesterday they escaped into the road when my dad was coming home from work. He ran over them and killed them (10 X 1%) all. He tried to miss them but he drove his car into the wall and broke his leg. (2%)  Because of that he lost his job (2%). I am so upset that I've got a terrible headache. (1%)

### 6 Speaking. With your partner think of some more exam excuses to go on the website. Here are some ideas for you: *you fell out of bed this morning; your cat was chased by a dog and you felt very frightened and stressed; your mother dropped a heavy box on her foot.* Tell your excuses to the class and try to look serious! Here are some expressions you can use.

> It was a terrible day yesterday...
> I'm feeling so stressed...
> I know it sounds silly but...
> I can't concentrate at all because...
> Please believe me...

### 7 Writing. Write your excuse to go on the website.

**Can-do checklist**

☐ **I can understand a personal letter describing feelings.**
☐ **I can understand factual information.**
☐ **I can talk and write about an imaginary past event.**
☐ **I can understand the description of an imaginary past event.**

# 27 PARDON?!

**1** Here are some words that only young people usually use in English. Match them with their meanings.

| | | | |
|---|---|---|---|
| **1** | very | **5** | great |
| **2** | horrible | **6** | great |
| **3** | good looking | **7** | great |
| **4** | things like gold jewellery | **8** | a bad thing |

> Cool! Wicked! Sad! Well good! Bad! Gross! Bling! Fit!

**2** Talk to a partner about these questions.

**1** Are there any new words in your language that you use but your parents don't? Can you give some examples?

**2** Do you know any words that are American English?

**3** Why do you think American English words are often used in Britain too?

**3** Read this introduction to a New Words Website. Do all new American English words come to England?

New words are born in America every day but not all of them cross the Atlantic and enter the British English dictionary. Here are some that will probably cross over soon!

**4** You are going to read some entries for new words on the site. Before reading, look at these words with your partner and see if you can guess what they mean.

| FREEGAN | FLEXITARIAN | SHOPGRIFTER | TWIXTER |
|---|---|---|---|

What sort of words usually end in –ER or –AN?

**5** Now read the entries and choose the correct words for the gaps.

**1** ........................... This is someone who buys an item of clothing on Friday, wears it to a party on Saturday and returns it to the shop on Monday for a refund. Sometimes people even buy big televisions to watch an important sports event and then return it the day after!

**2** ........................... This is someone who doesn't usually eat fish or meat because they think it's wrong but when it suits them they do! They usually say they don't eat meat and fish because it's quite fashionable in some places at the moment!

**3** ........................... This is someone who is between a child and an adult. This person has finished his/her education but hasn't got married, started a career or left home. There are more and more of these people these days. They often change jobs regularly, don't pay their parents rent and have quite a good time. Their parents aren't always happy about it!

**4** ........................... This is someone who is trying to protect the environment. He/she doesn't want to waste food so eats old bread, fruit and vegetables that supermarkets throw away. The supermarkets often give the food away free at the end of the week or sell it very cheaply.

**6** **Match the words to the pictures.**

**A** ........................................  **B** ........................................  **C** ........................................  **D** ........................................

**7** **Choose the correct answer A, B or C.**

**1** A shopgrifter
  **A)** takes something back because he/she doesn't like it.
  **B)** takes something back because they don't need it now.
  **C)** takes something back because it's faulty.

**2** A freegan
  **A)** hasn't got much money.
  **B)** likes old food.
  **C)** wants to help the environment.

**3** A twixter
  **A)** lives at home.
  **B)** goes to college.
  **C)** goes to work.

**4** A flexitarian
  **A)** never eats meat.
  **B)** always eats meat.
  **C)** sometimes eats meat.

**8** **Complete the gaps in the sentences with these words from the dictionary entries.**

| rent | waste | return | throw | suits | refund | protect |
|------|-------|--------|-------|-------|--------|---------|

**1** If you don't like something you've bought you can ........................ it.

**2** We can leave whenever it ........................ you.

**3** My friend has to pay her parents ........................ .

**4** At school children learn how to ........................ the environment.

**5** That shirt has a button missing. Ask for a ........................ .

**6** We ........................ so much food these days. It's terrible.

**7** That coat is very old. ........................ it away.

**9** **Look at these new words. They are made from two old words. Can you guess their meanings.**

**1** MOVIEOKE ................................................................

**2** BUSTITUTION ................................................................

**3** EGOSURFING ................................................................

**4** VOICE LIFT ................................................................

**5** PROTIRE ................................................................

Here are some clues.
KARAOKE
SUBSTITUTION
SURF THE NET
FACE LIFT
RETIRE

**10** **Speaking. With a partner try to make some new words from pairs of old words.**

e.g. An "umbrocket" could be an umbrella that fits into a pocket

**11** **Writing. Write the definitions for these entries on the New Word Website.**

**Can-do checklist**
☐ **I can recognise the significant points in a text.**
☐ **I can deduce the meaning of unfamiliar words.**
☐ **I can write detailed descriptions.**
☐ **I can give my opinion.**

# 28 CHEERS!

**1** **What is CHEERLEADING ?**

**2** **Do this quiz about cheerleading with your partner. Choose the answers A, B or C.**

1 Which country is famous for cheerleading?
**A)** England **B)** USA **C)** Italy
2 Who become cheerleaders?
**A)** Boys **B)** Girls **C)** both
3 Which sport is it associated with?
**A)** Tennis **B)** Swimming **C)** American Football
4 Today Cheerleading is mainly …
**A)** songs. **B)** dances. **C)** acrobatics.
5 To be a cheerleader you must be …
**A)** fit. **B)** flexible. **C)** good looking.
6 You can do cheerleading …
**A)** in a group. **B)** on your own. **C)** in either situation.
7 Cheerleaders usually wear …
**A)** pom poms. **B)** long skirts. **C)** lots of make up.

**3** **Read this article in a magazine about cheerleading. Is there anything that surprises you about it?**

## ✱✱✱✱✱✱✱ Cheerleading ✱✱✱✱✱✱✱

**1** .............................
I used to think that cheerleading was a very American thing. It happened at American football matches and there were rows of pretty girls in short skirts with pom poms in their hands jumping up and down and shouting stuff like "Go – cowboys – Go!!!"

**2** .............................
How wrong was I?! Cheerleading in the 21st century is much more serious. For teenagers in many countries it's a hobby, a sport – almost a way of life. At the

International Cheerleading Championships 150 teams compete, and winning the competition is the most important thing in these young people's lives. It is also extremely expensive – up to £2,000 a year for each cheerleader.

**3** .............................
So, what is cheerleading? Today, it is a form of team acrobatics to hip-hop music. The members of the teams are all excellent gymnasts and their routines are complicated. Some of the team,

called "flyers" are thrown as high into the air as possible by the "bases". Both boys and girls can be cheerleaders. The boys throw and the girls fly!

**4** .............................
It is quite amazing to watch a cheerleading team. As part of the show the girls wear a lot of make up and ribbons in their hair. The audience cheer, whistle and ring bells. It's very noisy, very exciting and very competitive. As one girl said: "It isn't a matter of life and death. It's MUCH more serious!"

**4** **Choose the correct headings to go with each paragraph.**

**A** Quite a show **B** Expensive competition **C** Only in America **D** Not just pretty faces

**5** **Match these words from the text to the pictures.**

| whistle | audience | team | pom poms | make-up | ribbons |

**6** **Are the following statements true or false? Circle T or F.**

1 Cheerleaders always have pom poms.       T  F
2 It costs a lot to be a cheerleader.           T  F
3 Cheerleaders use music.                       T  F
4 Both boys and girls wear make up.            T  F
5 The audience is usually quiet.                T  F
6 The competitions are good and it's OK to lose.  T  F

**7** **Talk to a partner about these questions.**

1 Do you think people in your area would like to have a cheerleading team? Why/not?
2 What is your national sport and do you support it?
3 Do you know any special chants used at sporting events in your country?

**8** **Here are some words often used in cheerleaders' chants. Match them with their meanings.**

chant                          put your hands together
clap                               shout very loudly
tough                          a short rhythmic poem
stomp                                       strong
beat            put your foot on the ground loudly
yell         hit, e.g. your leg with your hand loudly
slap                                  be the winner

**9** **Speaking. Look at these chants. One group practise chanting A and one group practise B. Who are the best chanters?**

We heard it from some people
That your team is really tough
But when you're up against [THE CHIEFS]
Tough is not enough!
(Stomp right foot. Clap.
Stomp right foot twice. Clap.
Stomp left foot twice. Clap)

**A**

THE CHIEFS are here
Stand up, now cheer!
We're here for some fun
We're number one!
We're at the top
We can't be stopped!
THE CHIEFS on top!
THE CHIEFS we rock!

**B**

**10** **Writing. With your partner choose a name for a team. Now try to write a short chant.**

**Can-do checklist**

☐ **I can find relevant information in an article.**
☐ **I can write a short poem.**
☐ **I can ask for and give opinion.**
☐ **I can understand the significant points in a text.**

# 29 A SONG FOR EUROPE?

**1** **Talk to a partner about these questions.**

1 What is the Eurovision Song Contest?
2 How often can we watch it?
3 Do you watch it? Why/not?
4 Why do you think it is so popular?
5 Can you remember any songs from the last contest?
6 When did your country last win?

**2** **Can you answer the questions in this Eurovision Quiz. If you don't know the answers, just guess and see who is closest to the right answers.**

1 When did the contest begin? ....................................................................................................
2 What nationality was the person who started the contest? ....................................................
3 Who won the first three contests? ..........................................................................................
4 Which group won with "Waterloo"? .......................................................................................
5 What nationality were they? ...................................................................................................
6 What was the original title of "Waterloo"? ............................................................................
7 In which month is the contest usually held? ..........................................................................
8 How many countries enter the contest? .................................................................................
9 How many people watch the contest? ....................................................................................
10 Which country has won most often? ......................................................................................

**3** **Read this internet news report about the Eurovision Song Contest and answer the question after it.**

### A party for Europe!

Last night Europe watched singers from 39 countries sing their hearts out to win the title of "Best Song in Europe". Once again, we saw all types of music from ballads to glam rock. There were also all sorts of singers – solo artists, boybands, duos and for the first time there was even a grandmother on stage, playing a drum! It was a great night. Perhaps not all the music was of a high standard but the atmosphere at the Contest was like a big, big party. Both the singers and the audience were enthusiastic and there was a lot of clapping and cheering for every song. The clothes were glamorous and sometimes outrageous, and the stage and lighting spectacular. All in all this looked and felt like a huge party for Europe where all nationalities came together and had great fun.

Is this report **a)** positive **b)** negative ?

**4** **Label this picture with these words from the report.**

stage   audience   drum   solo artist   duo   clapping   cheering   glam rock

**5** **Representatives from each country give their votes for the songs. Here are some things they said to the presenters of the show.**

*A Congratulations on a wonderful evening.*

*B Well done. It's been a great show.*

*C We would like to congratulate you on a very professional production.*

**1** Which expression in bold is
  **1** very formal?   **2** quite formal?   **3** informal?
**2** Which expression would these people use?
  **1** a friend   **2** your grandmother   **3** headteacher at a prize giving.

**6** **With your partner choose a song for Europe for your country.**

**1** Choose a title.
**2** Choose the type of song.
**3** Choose a singer/singers.
**4** Choose clothes.
**5** Choose a dance.
**6** Choose any special effects.

**7** **Speaking. Tell your class about your song and singer/s. Listen to the other suggestions and then with your partner talk about the songs and choose one of them. Then vote on the different songs. Each pair represents a different town or area of your country and says:** *And here are the results of the ............... jury!*

Here are some expressions to use when making choices or decisions together.

*What about ...?*
*I like the idea of ...*
*I think we should go for ...*
*What do you think about ...?*
*Let's make a choice.*
*But don't you think ...?*
*I think you're right.*
*Good choice!*

**8** **Writing. Imagine your song won the Eurovision last night. Write a short report for an internet site.**

**Can-do checklist**

☐ **I can identify the writer's opinion.**
☐ **I can understand differences between formal and informal language.**
☐ **I can write about a past event.**
☐ **I can talk about choices.**

# 30 SCENT-SITIVE?

**1** **Talk to a partner about these questions.**

1 What are your favourite smells?
2 Do smells make you remember different times?
3 What smells do you hate?
4 Do you have a strong sense of smell?

**2** **Do this quiz with your partner.**

### QUIZ

1 Why can't we taste things if we hold our nose?
2 How many smell cells do dogs have in their noses?
 **a)** 500,000 **b)** 2,000,000
3 Humans have a special chemical that keeps insects away. **True** or **False**?
4 How many smells can humans tell the difference between?
 **a)** 4,000 **b)** 15,000
5 How many different types of smell are there?
 **a)** 7 **b)** 25 **c)** 53

**3** **You are going to read two leaflets about a new form of advertising. Read both leaflets and answer the questions after them.**

---

#### LEAFLET A

# Have your say

This shop is thinking about using a new form of advertising and we hope you will give us your views. Today we are having an experiment. As you walk through the supermarket you will notice different smells in different places. We hope this will be a pleasant experience for you.

When you finish your shopping, we would be very grateful if you could complete the questionnaire at the bottom of this leaflet.

This is YOUR supermarket. Please tell us YOUR views. Have YOUR say!

1 Would you like to have different smells in a supermarket? ....................
2 Which of these smells would you like to have in a supermarket? roast lamb, flowers, lemon, garlic, cheese, chocolate, curry ..............................
3 Which of the smells would you not like to have in a supermarket? ..................
4 Can you add any more smells that might be suitable for a supermarket?..........................
5 If we had these smells in this supermarket, would you come in more often or less often? ...........................

**Please e-mail any comments to www.21centuryad.com**

---

# SAY NO!

Do we really want smelly shops? This is all to help companies sell more products. Scientists say that the senses of taste and smell are very closely connected. If we drink some water from a bottle that smells of lemon, we think that the water tastes of lemon. The sense of smell goes directly to the emotional part of the brain and NOT to the thinking part. Because of this, some advertisers want to put smells in the packaging of products. This means that when we walk past the meat shelves, we can smell sausages or roast lamb. When we walk past cleaning products, we can smell lemon or flowers! They want to persuade us to buy more. Is this what you want? Advertisers have a lot of power already. Do we really want them to attack us through our noses?

#### LEAFLET B

# SAY NO!

The writer of which leaflet

1 thinks smell advertising is a good idea? **A** **B**
2 wants to know what we think? **A** **B**
3 wants to please customers? **A** **B**
4 wants to try something new? **A** **B**
5 gives us some scientific information? **A** **B**
6 thinks this idea is only about making money? **A** **B**

**4** **Read the leaflets again to complete these sentences.**

1 We are thinking ..................... using a new form of advertising.

2 Today we are ..................... an experiment in this shop.

3 We would be very ..................... if you could complete this questionnaire.

4 We ..................... this will be a pleasant experience for you.

5 The bottle smells ..................... lemon.

6 When we walk ..................... the meat shelves we can smell sausages.

7 Do we want them to attack us ..................... our noses?!

**5** Match these words to the things in the picture.

sausages    cleaning products    shelf    garlic    packaging    lemon

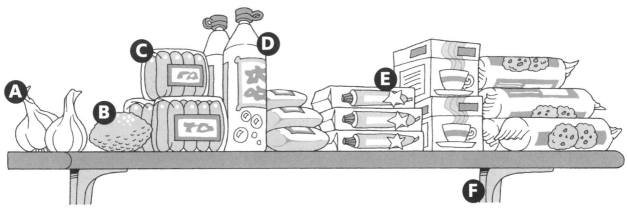

**6** Answer the questionnaire in leaflet A with your partner.

**7** Speaking. Here are some more shops. Talk about what smells they could have to advertise their goods.

**8** Writing. Send an e-mail to the manager of the supermarket explaining why you think it is a good/bad idea to have smell advertising.

**Can-do checklist**

☐ I can identify the writer's opinion.
☐ I can use a questionnaire.
☐ I can ask for and give personal information.
☐ I can read a leaflet for main information.

# TEST 3 READING

## Part 1   Questions 1–5

Look at the text in each question. Circle the correct answer A, B, C or D.

**1**  Where can you read this?

> All the clues down begin with the letter D.

A  in a detective novel
B  in the rules for a card game
C  in the rules for a word puzzle

**2**  Where would you see this?

> You can't beat it.
> **Three** courses for only **£10!**

A  by the sea
B  outside a restaurant
C  at a sports event

**3**  What will the shop do?

> *Return an item within one week
> and we'll give you a full refund.*

A  They will give you another item.
B  They will exchange items after a week.
C  They will give you your money back in the first week.

**4**  What do you do?

> **Phone this number to record your vote.**

A  Choose a record.
B  Tell someone your choice on the phone.
C  Send someone your phone number.

**5**  Who would write this?

> PLEASE INCLUDE A SAMPLE OF YOUR
> HANDWRITING WITH YOUR APPLICATION.

A  a graphologist
B  a company
C  a doctor

## Part 2   Questions 6–10

These people want to go to a music festival. Decide who will go to which festival.

**6**  Mandy is 13 and loves boy bands and sing-along music. She likes dancing and isn't keen on slow songs.

**7**  Penny is 18 and is very romantic. She likes songs that are about love and have good words. She doesn't like music without words.

**8**  Dave Parker is 56 and likes old fashioned rock 'n' roll. He always turns his music up loud.

**9**  Dave's wife Em is 52. She plays folk songs on her guitar. She doesn't like female singers.

**10**  Brent is 25 and loves clubbing and electronic dance music. He likes music which some people think is repetitive with a strong beat.

**A**  Craig Peters is a dark haired, blue eyed Irish ballad singer. He's 19 with a lovely voice and sings sad love songs.

**B**  Boy Wonder is a duo made up of Mark and Pete. They sing traditional songs with acoustic guitars and Irish whistles.

**C**  The Beanie Boys are made up of Gary, Jon, Dave, Jed and Robbie. They sing easy listening pop music. Their songs are very catchy.

**D**  Car Wash is a team of dancers and a DJ. They're very flexible and dance to their music with spectacular lighting effects.

**E**  The Stompers is a group of lads from Liverpool who recreate the heavy beats of the 60s with their guitars and drums. Ideal for aging rockers.

## Part 3  Questions 11–20

Look at the sentences below about a day in the life of Jem Tyler. Read the extract to decide if the sentences are true or false.

| | | |
|---|---|---|
| **11** | Jem had worked hard for this exam. | **T  F** |
| **12** | He got up early to do some exercise. | **T  F** |
| **13** | The alarm clock woke him up at the wrong time. | **T  F** |
| **14** | He hurt his head and his hand. | **T  F** |
| **15** | His sister made him wet. | **T  F** |
| **16** | He couldn't study in his bedroom. | **T  F** |
| **17** | He went back to bed for some more sleep. | **T  F** |
| **18** | Jem made breakfast. | **T  F** |
| **19** | His sisters made him late for the bus. | **T  F** |
| **20** | The exam questions were too difficult for him. | **T  F** |

Jem Tyler had a really bad day last Thursday. It was the day of his last summer exam and he was slightly worried as he wasn't very well prepared. Because of this he set his alarm to wake him up at five in the morning so that he could do some revision before the exam which started at 9.30.

The alarm woke him up and he sat up very quickly, turned over and fell out of bed. He hurt his head on the table. It was still dark and he went to the bathroom but banged his toe on the door in the darkness. He shouted so loudly that he woke up his younger sister in the next room. She was angry and threw a glass of water over him. Then he realised that he'd made a mistake with the alarm clock and it wasn't 5 o'clock but 4 o'clock. He went to study at his table in the bedroom but the light wasn't working so he went downstairs. He read his books for five minutes in the kitchen but he was so tired he went to sleep at the kitchen table and didn't wake up until his mother came to make breakfast for the family. It was too noisy to work then. He couldn't get into the bathroom because of his sisters and he missed the bus to school. He arrived half an hour late for the exam and they refused to allow him to take it. What a disaster!

## Part 4   Questions 21–25

Read the text and questions below.
For each question circle the correct letter – A, B, C or D.

**21** "Peaches"
  A  is a brand new restaurant.
  B  has a brand new chef.
  C  has a brand new menu.

**22** The writer thought
  A  the food made him thirsty.
  B  the food upset his taste buds.
  C  the food was very good indeed.

**23**  In the restaurant
  A  there were famous people.
  B  there were millionaires.
  C  there were other chefs.

**24**  The restaurant also had
  A  famous paintings on the walls.
  B  free perfume for the guests.
  C  soft music.

**25**  The writer recommends the restaurant
  A  to everyone.
  B  to rich people.
  C  to people with too much time.

## A taste of "Peaches"

What an incredible experience! Last night I had the pleasure of going to the opening of the new "Peaches" restaurant in High Street, Oakton and, together with celebrities, reviewers and people from the media, I ate my way through a six course meal with aperitifs, wines and liqueurs. From the mouthwatering soup and patés to the delicious cheeses and desserts, it was a food festival of absolute excellence and my congratulations go to the chef and owner Paddy Taggart. He has created a "sense spectacular" in "Peaches". There is the superb food for our tongues, delicate scents in the air, gentle spiritual music to accompany the meal and all in a room so beautifully designed that it was like sitting in an impressionist painting! I would advise anyone who is looking for delicious food in stunning surroundings to book a table at "Peaches" – anyone who has a lot of money and a lot of time. You cannot eat here if you are in a hurry!

# 31 FUNHOUSE

**1** **Talk to a partner about these questions.**

1 What is a "gadget"?
   **A)** something you keep in the fridge
   **B)** a type of picture
   **C)** something small and clever that makes jobs easier
2 Do you have any gadgets in your house? What?
3 What gadgets would you like to have?

**2** **Here are some things we may find in the "houses of the future". Which are shown in the picture? Number each of them.**

1 electronic taps ☐
2 a machine that washes, dries and irons clothes ☐
3 a phone that tells you who is calling ☐
4 a waterproof entertainment system in the bathroom ☐
5 a steam room with CD player ☐
6 an eco friendly waste system ☐
7 room to room intercom ☐
8 electronic changing pictures ☐
9 windows that clean themselves ☐
10 curtains that open and close when you tell them ☐
11 self cleaning carpets ☐

**3** (25) **Listen to this phone conversation and tick which of the above things are mentioned.**

**4** **Why is the family spending time in this house?**

   **A)** They won a prize.   **B)** They bought the house.   **C)** It's a sort of test.

**5** **Which of these sentences are true for A) Abby   B) Brian   C) neither**

1 I would love to live in a house like this.   **A   B   C**
2 I would like to spend some time in a house like this.   **A   B   C**
3 I would never spend time in a house like this.   **A   B   C**
4 I think this house is amazing.   **A   B   C**
5 I don't understand some of these gadgets.   **A   B   C**

**6** **Match these words and expressions from the conversation with the meanings.**

| | |
|---|---|
| 1 Weird | A) I would go crazy. |
| 2 After a while | B) You're joking! |
| 3 That's a relief | C) Strange! |
| 4 Can you imagine? | D) Soon |
| 5 You're kidding! | E) Thank goodness! |
| 6 It would do my head in! | F) Isn't that fantastic? |

Give your partner a situation to respond to using one of the expressions.

**7** (25) **Listen again. How does Abby explain these things?**

**1** hi-tech ..............................................................................................................................................

**2** waterproof ........................................................................................................................................

**3** weather monitor ...............................................................................................................................

Would you like to have these gadgets in your house? Why/not?

What do you think it would be like to live in a house like this?

**8** **Speaking. With your partner think of some more gadgets you could have in a "house of the future". Give them names.**

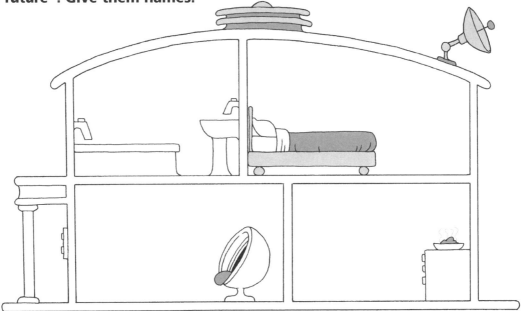

**9** **Change partners and tell your new partner about these ideas. Here are some expressions that Brian used when he didn't understand. Use some of these in your conversations.**

What do you mean "a..."?

Sorry – you've lost me!

Waterproof?

Why "intercom"?

I don't follow.

**10** **Writing. Write a paragraph about your "house of the future". Begin:** *In my house of the future there will be ...*

**Can-do checklist**
- [ ] **I can ask for clarification.**
- [ ] **I can compensate for not knowing the meaning of a word.**
- [ ] **I can write a short description.**
- [ ] **I can understand a speaker's point of view.**

# 32 SHOPPING PLANS

**1** **Use this shopping survey with your group.**

1 How often do you go clothes shopping?
2 How long do you usually spend shopping for clothes?
3 Who do you usually go with?
4 What is your favourite shop for clothes? Why?

5 Which new item of clothing you have bought do you like best?
6 Is there any item you would really like to buy soon?
7 Do you throw away old clothes when you buy new ones?
8 Do you have a big wardrobe?

**2** **Find twelve different types of clothing in this wordsearch, e.g. sports wear.**

```
A C A S U A L L E
S T O U N F I N E
U O U T D O O R N
M E M F E O T H I
M S P O R T S N G
E M A R W O R K H
R A R M E P L I T
T R T A A L O D E
Y T Y L R I N S S
```

**3** **Match the words in italics in these sentences to the pictures.**

1 The new *layout* of the shop is very modern and attractive.
2 You have to pay at the *cash desk*.
3 You'll look great at the party with those clothes. You need some *accessories* to make you look perfect.
4 Go and try these jeans on in the *changing rooms*.
5 The sales are on and all the shops are *packed out* – it's horrendous!

**4** 🎧 **Listen to a clothes shop manager talking to his staff about a new layout for the shop. Tick which of the types of clothing in activity 2 he talks about.**

**5** **Answer these questions.**

1 Why do they need to change the layout of the shop? ...........................................................................

2 Is the clothes shop for boys, girls or both? ...........................................................................

**6** (26) **Listen again and look at the plan for the new layout. Fill in the different sections.**

Bags ☐

Hats and scarves ☐

Jewellery ☐

Male body products ☐

Girls' underwear ☐

Girls' partywear ☐

Girls' casual wear ☐

Men's outdoorwear ☐

Men's partywear ☐

Men's smartwear ☐

Men's footwear ☐

Changing rooms ☐

Cash desk ☐

**M**
**L**
**D**
Girls' footwear
Men's casual wear
**J**
Girls' nightwear
**K**
**I**
Girls' smartwear
**B**
Men's underwear
**H**
Kids' section
**G**
**C**
**E**
Belts
**F**
Make-up
Male jewellery
**A**

**7** **In which section of the shop would you look for these items?**

1  Ladies' trainers
2  A nightdress
3  Men's pyjamas

4  A bikini
5  A long dress for a special occasion
6  A ring for your girlfriend

7  Men's body lotion
8  A coat for your 6-year-old brother
9  A Gucci handbag

**8** **Here are some things that can make a shop more attractive to customers. Talk to your partner about why these things can attract people to a shop and then decide which two you think are most important.**

music

bargain area

more choice

good changing rooms

posters

play area for children

more assistants

**9** **Speaking. Using a blank sheet of paper, design your own shop. Tell your partner where the different things are. Here are some expressions that the manager used when he was talking to his staff. Use some of them when you tell your partner about the layout of your shop.**

in front of
behind
next to
the whole back section
bang in the centre
on the right
on the left

**10** **Writing. Write a paragraph describing your shop.**

**Can-do checklist**

☐ **I can understand directions.**
☐ **I can write a detailed description.**
☐ **I can use a questionnaire/survey.**
☐ **I can ask for and give personal information.**

# 33 MUSIC MUSIC

**1** **Talk to a partner about these questions.**

1 Have you ever been to an open-air music festival?
2 Who would you most like to see at a music festival?
3 Are there any famous music festivals in your area?
4 How long do music festivals last usually?
5 What sort of things can you buy at festivals?

**2** **Read the words in the musical notes. Match them with the words in italics in the sentences. Write the number of the sentence in the other half of the note.**

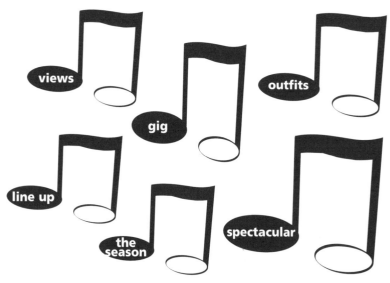

views
outfits
gig
line up
the season
spectacular

1 Summer is *the time* when most festivals take place.
2 The stage at the concert last night looked *amazing* with all the lights, singers, dancers and everything.
3 My parents and I do not have the same *opinions* about music!
4 My favourite band is doing a *concert* at the Town Hall. I can't wait!
5 You've got to come to the concert on Saturday. Look at the *list of singers* – it will be incredible.
6 The lead singer always wears really strange *clothes*.

**3** **You are going to listen to the "Festival News" section of a radio programme. Tick which points you think the presenter will talk about.**

| | | | | | |
|---|---|---|---|---|---|
| Dates | ☐ ☐ | Ticket prices | ☐ ☐ | Stars | ☐ ☐ |
| Places | ☐ ☐ | CDs | ☐ ☐ | Contact numbers | ☐ ☐ |

**4** 🎧 **(27) Listen to the "Festival News" on the radio and tick which the presenter actually talks about.**

**5** **Complete these phrases from the radio programme.**

1 The ......................... season is coming.
2 The ......................... news at the moment is that …
3 Britney is ......................... this summer.
4 She's ......................... Bristol, Oxford and Exeter.
5 She's spending a ......................... .
6 The weather ......................... is good.
7 So, get ......................... and reserve your space.

**6** (27) **Listen again and complete the information in the table.**

| STAR | PLACE | TIME |
|------|-------|------|
|      |       |      |
|      |       |      |
|      |       |      |

**7** With your partner ask and answer questions about the festival information in activity 6. Use question words such as: *who/where/when*.

**8** Speaking. With your partner make arrangements to go to a festival. Discuss these questions:

*Where will you meet?*
*How will you travel?*
*When will you meet?*
*Who will you go with?*
*How long will you stay?*

*Will you take a tent?*
*What else will you take?*
*What will you wear?*
*What's the forecast?*
*How much are the tickets?*

**9** Now change partners. Phone your new partner to give information about the arrangements. There is a slight problem – it is a bad phone line/signal and your partner can't hear the important information so he/she must ask you questions.

Use question words:
*Who/Where/When/What/How long/How much*

We're going to meet at... <crackle>

At the station...

Where are we going to meet?

**10** Writing. Write an e-mail to your friend giving the information about the arrangements.

**Can-do checklist**
- ☐ I can ask for repetition.
- ☐ I can correct confusion.
- ☐ I can make arrangements orally and in writing.
- ☐ I can ask for and give clarification.

# 34 THE BALLAD OF JEN AND STANLEY

**1** Here are some adjectives English teenagers use to describe other people. Which are positive and which are negative? Put them into the correct columns.

> loser    dull    plastic    freaky
> weirdo    wicked    classy    superstar
> diamond    doughnut    fake    boring
> amazing    cool    sassy    cringey    creepy

| ☺ POSITIVE | ☹ NEGATIVE |
|---|---|
|  |  |
|  |  |
|  |  |
|  |  |
|  |  |
|  |  |
|  |  |
|  |  |
|  |  |
|  |  |
|  |  |

**2** How many of these words can you find in the wordsearch?

```
A D R O S I P A L
C I N D U L L M E
O A S I P W A A I
O M A N E I S Z C
L O S E R C T I L
A N S E S K I N A
I D Y L T E C G S
F A K E A D E S S
E N D C R E E P Y
```

**3** Discuss with a partner. What are the advantages and disadvantages of having a car or a mountain bike?

| Mountain Bike | |
|---|---|
| **ADVANTAGES** | **DISADVANTAGES** |
|  |  |

| Car | |
|---|---|
| **ADVANTAGES** | **DISADVANTAGES** |
|  |  |

**4** 🔊28 Listen to "The ballad of Jen and Stanley" and circle which of the words from activity 1 you hear.

**5** **Put these pictures of the ballad into the correct order.**

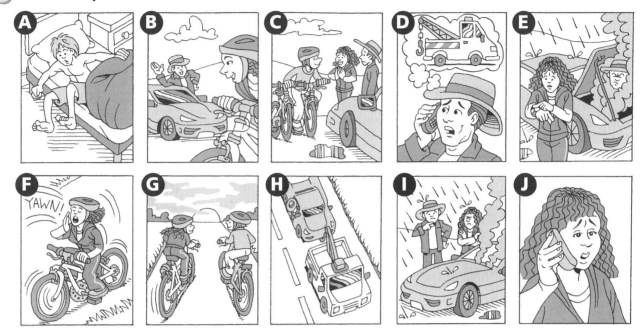

**6** 🎧 **Listen again and complete the pairs of rhyming words.**

1 was ................................................

2 like ................................................

3 day ................................................

4 bother ................................................

5 Matt ................................................

6 Ferrari ................................................

7 manly ................................................

8 wet ................................................

9 ten ................................................

10 do ................................................

11 said ................................................

12 phoning ................................................

13 train ................................................

14 Stan ................................................

15 this ................................................

16 hand ................................................

17 hill ................................................

18 home ................................................

19 see ................................................

**7** **Speaking. With your partner find words that rhyme with the following:**

1 stand ........................

2 car ........................

3 tree ........................

4 hair ........................

5 sing ........................

6 boy ........................

7 sun ........................

8 cat ........................

9 sky ........................

10 stay ........................

11 fine ........................

12 phone ........................

**8** **Writing. Choose some of these rhyming pairs and write a short ballad with your partner.**

**Can-do checklist**

☐ **I can understand the narrative of a poem.**

☐ **I can understand and use descriptive words.**

☐ **I can write a simple poem.**

☐ **I can summarise a story.**

# 35 PARTYTIME

**1** **Talk to a partner about these questions.**

1 What is the best party you can remember?
2 What can go wrong at a party?
3 What is a "gatecrasher"?
4 What do you think "having an empty" means?
5 Do your parents ever go away and leave you at home?
6 If your parents were away, would you think about having a party?
7 Have you ever been to a party at a friend's house while his/her parents were away?

**2** **Complete the sentences with these prepositions.**

| at | on | up | for | in | over | about |

1 We wanted to have something different to eat but we ended ...................... with pizza as usual.
2 Our teacher is very hard ...................... students who don't do their homework.
3 I left my dog ...................... his own for the afternoon while I went shopping.
4 I always feel guilty ...................... buying chocolates!
5 My brother's really good ...................... running.
6 My mother always says she won't let us have any more fast food but she always gives ...................... !
7 Every time I go to the café with Robbie I end up paying ...................... the drinks.
8 We often invite friends ...................... to watch a DVD.

**3** (29) **You are going to listen to a radio discussion about 'empties' and sleepovers. Listen to the discussion and circle the answers to the questions: Dave (D), Mary (M) or both (B).**

**WHO ...**

| | | | |
|---|---|---|---|
| 1 has a ten year old daughter? | D | M | B |
| 2 went to Spain? | D | M | B |
| 3 had a bad night? | D | M | B |
| 4 has a sixteen year old son? | D | M | B |
| 5 had to pay a lot of money? | D | M | B |
| 6 had to take a friend home during the night? | D | M | B |
| 7 had a messed up house? | D | M | B |
| 8 had drunk people in their house? | D | M | B |
| 9 had six of their child's friends in their house? | D | M | B |
| 10 doesn't want their child to have friends over again? | D | M | B |

**4** 🎧 **Listen again and answer these questions.**

1 What's the name of David's son? ........................................................................................

2 What's the name of Mary's daughter? ................................................................................

3 What did the kids smash in David's house? .......................................................................

4 Why did Mary have to take a child home in the middle of the night? ..............................

5 Why couldn't Mary or her husband sleep that night? .......................................................

6 How many children does Mary have? ................................................................................

7 How many children does David have? ...............................................................................

8 How many children does the presenter have? ...................................................................

**5** **Speaking. With your partner talk about what different parties people can have. Write down as many words as you can in these different categories.**

PLACE

MUSIC

CLOTHES

TYPE OF PARTY

FOOD

**6** **In groups of eight get a piece of paper to make up a party. Write a type of party on the first line then fold over the paper and pass it on. Write the time and date on the second line, fold, pass on etc., until the papers are filled. The person who completes the last line reads out the completed invitations.**

Please come to my ......    We will drink ......

On (date and time) ......    The music will be ......

At (place) ......    Please wear ......

We will eat......    We will also ......

**7** **Speaking. Have a conversation with your partner about a party. It can be a brilliant party or one where things went wrong. Use some of the turn-taking expressions.**

**8** **Writing. Write a short account of a fun party you went to.**

What about you?
And you?
Why did...?
Will you ever ....?
What happened to you?
What do you think?

**Can-do checklist**

☐ **I can understand an extended discussion.**

☐ **I can use turn taking in a conversation.**

☐ **I can understand specific information.**

☐ **I can use collocations (with prepositions).**

# 36 I'M SEEING THINGS

**1** Use these clues to complete the word puzzles and find the mystery words.

**A**

**1** It's not a real person, it's a .......... .
**2** The noun from to die.
**3** A manservant.
**4** Marks where blood has dropped.
**5** A country of the UK.
**6** He .......... him with a knife.
**7** He didn't die by accident. It was .......... .

**B**

**1** A small stone area outside a house.
**2** When you enter a house you go into the .......... .
**3** To go upstairs in a big house you use the .......... .
**4** The cook works in this room.
**5** A room for dancing in an old house.
**6** Where you sleep.

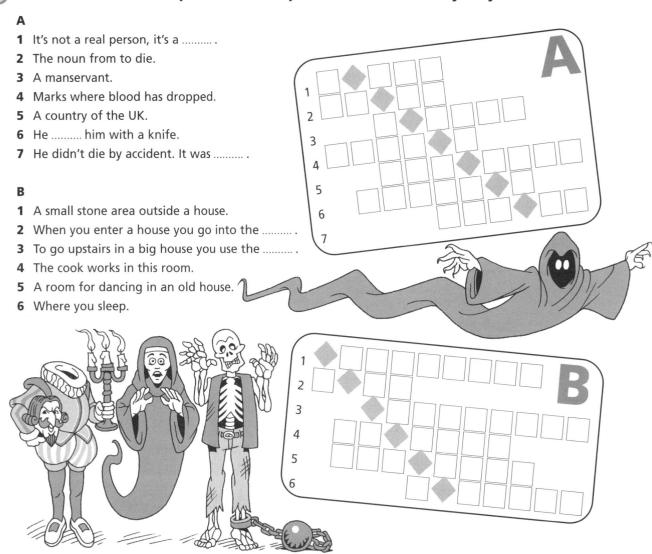

**2** **(30)** You are going to listen to a tour guide recording for visitors to a castle. One of the words from the crosswords is not in the recording. Which one?

**3** In pairs, write down one thing you can SEE in the castle, one thing you can HEAR, one thing you can SMELL and one thing you can FEEL. Compare your answers with another pair.

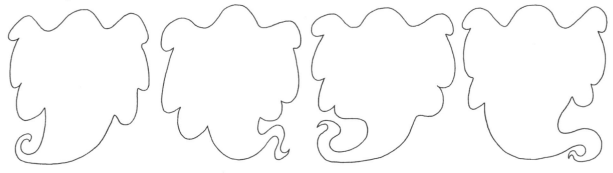

**4** 🎧 **Listen again and put these people in the different places.**

| | | | |
|---|---|---|---|
| Martha Dooley | Jarvis | Grandmother Frances | Elizabeth and George |
| The traveller | The violinist | Agnes | Lord and Lady Carver |

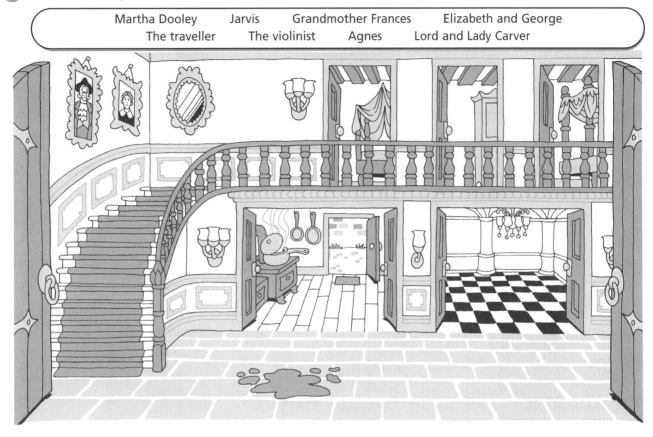

**5** **Complete this table.**

| WHO | HOW DIED | WHY DIED |
|---|---|---|
| Jarvis | | |
| Lord and Lady Carver | | |
| Grandmother Frances | | |
| Elizabeth and George | | |
| The traveller | | |
| The violinist | | |

**6** **Speaking. With your partner invent some new ghosts to put in the castle. Think of HOW they died and WHERE and WHY. Change partners and give a short new tour guide so that he/she can put in the new ghosts with the information.**

**7** **Writing. Write the new entries for the castle brochure.**

**Can-do checklist**
- ☐ **I can follow and give directions.**
- ☐ **I can talk about the different senses.**
- ☐ **I can talk about an imaginary event.**
- ☐ **I can write a brochure entry.**

# 37 MY BIG FOOT

**1** **Make as many words as you can from:**

# EMBARRASSED

**2** **Complete the sentences with these words and find some more expressions connected with embarrassment.**

> cringe    red    foot    think

**1** When I realised he was listening to every word I said about him, I went so ................... .

**2** He must learn to ................... before he speaks. He always says embarrassing things!

**3** I always ................... when my mum starts singing! It's so awful.

**4** I really put my ................... in it yesterday when I told him I'd seen his girlfriend at a party.

**3** **Talk to a partner about these questions.**

**1** Can you think of some examples of situations when people "go red"?

**2** Have you ever "put your foot in it"? What happened?

**4**  **You are going to listen to two phone conversations where someone puts their foot in it! Listen and answer the questions.**

**In conversation A**

1 Who answers the phone?

......................................................

2 Why does she answer the phone?

......................................................

3 Who does the caller ask for?

......................................................

4 What is the mistake?

......................................................

5 What makes the conversation so embarrassing?

......................................................

**In conversation B**

1 Who is phoning? ................................

2 Who does he think he is speaking to?

......................................................

3 Why is he phoning? ...........................

4 Why does he think he has the wrong number?

......................................................

5 Who is he speaking to? ......................

**5** **What do you think Kathy and Jake do or say at the end of these phone calls?**

**A)** hang up   **B)** apologise

🎧 **32** **Listen to the rest of the calls.**

Were you right?!

**6** **Here are some expressions you can use if you put your foot in it.**

> I am SO sorry.
> I thought you were …
> I can't believe I just did that.
> I can't believe I just said that.

**And here are some to respond to the situation.**

> That's OK.
> Don't worry about it!
> It's a common mistake.
> That was an awful thing to do/say.
> I never want to see you/speak to you again!
> I can't believe you just did that.
> I can't believe you just said that.

**7** **Speaking. Phone your partner. Take it in turns to use these situations. At the end of the call you can hang up, apologise and/or explain.**

**1** You think you're talking to your friend. You talk about a wild party you went to last night. It's his/her sister/brother.

**2** You think you're talking to your girl/boyfriend. You talk about what a great time you had last night. You've dialled the wrong number. It's your ex.

**3** You think you're talking to your friend. You talk about what happened today when you both had to go to see the headteacher about your behaviour. It's his/her father/mother.

**8** **Writing. Choose one of the situations from the listening or speaking and write an e-mail to another friend explaining the embarrassing situation and what you said and did.**

---

**Can-do checklist**

☐ **I can apologise and respond to an apology.**
☐ **I can use phone language.**
☐ **I can identify specific information.**
☐ **I can use lexis connected with embarrassment.**

# 38 LOVE IT OR HATE IT?

**1** **Work in groups and answer the questions in this survey.**

1 Do you have a favourite ringtone?
2 Is there a ringtone you hate?
3 How often do you change your ringtone?
4 Do you like ringtones from popular songs?
5 How often do you buy CDs?
6 What was the last CD that you bought?
7 What's your favourite CD?
8 Do you buy CDs or do you download?
9 Do you prefer real music or electronic music?
10 Do you like the same music as your parents?

**2** **Put these adjectives into the different columns.**

catchy
irritating
wicked
electronic
different
repetitive
moronic
demented
new
brill

| POSITIVE | NEGATIVE | EITHER |
|---|---|---|
|  |  |  |
|  |  |  |
|  |  |  |
|  |  |  |

**3** **Match these statements with the pictures.**

**A)** It's number 1.     **B)** It's a trend.     **C)** It drives me nuts.     **D)** It's his tummy button.

**4** 🎧 33 **Listen to this part of a radio programme and answer this question.**

Why is the Crazy Frog song unusual?

**5** Who says these things? Circle S for Sadie, M for Maria, T for Ted. Sometimes you need to circle more than one.

1 Older people don't like it.                  S   M   T
2 There have been strange records before.      S   M   T
3 It's a wonderful song.                        S   M   T
4 You hear it everywhere.                       S   M   T
5 The frog is the wrong colour.                 S   M   T
6 Pop music is not for adults.                  S   M   T
7 I don't want to listen to it.                 S   M   T

**6** 🎧 33 Listen again. Which singers do they mention?

1 Sadie    **A)** Madonna      **B)** Elvis    **C)** Abba
2 Maria    **A)** Cold Play    **B)** Travis   **C)** The Coral
3 Ted      **A)** The Beatles  **B)** Queen    **C)** Kylie Minogue

**7** Speaking. Talk to a partner about these questions.

1 What do you like or do that drives your parents nuts?
2 What do your parents like or do that drives you nuts?

Here are some expressions to express your feelings. Use some of them in your conversation.

It's really awful!
It makes me want to scream!
I can't stand it!
It's so boring!
I get so embarrassed!

**8** Writing. Write some sentences about the differences between what you and your parents like/dislike. Look at this model. *I love watching reality TV but my parents can't stand it.*

**Can-do checklist**
☐ **I can talk and write about differences.**
☐ **I can use contrastive link words.**
☐ **I can express negative reactions.**
☐ **I can use a questionnaire.**

# 39 DREAM JOB

**1** **What jobs can you have working for a magazine? First match these activities with the jobs in the pictures.**

**1** I take pictures of famous people.
**2** I give advice on medical problems.
**3** I try out new make up.
**4** I write reviews of new music.
**5** I wear new clothes to show the readers.
**6** I interview people.
**7** I arrange the pictures and articles on the pages.

**A** ........................ **B** ........................ **C** ........................

**Then label the pictures with the correct jobs.**

journalist     reviewer
tester     model
photographer     doctor
designer

**D** ........................ **E** ........................ **F** ........................ **G** ........................

**2** **Talk to a partner about these questions.**

**1** Would you like any of these jobs? Why/not?
**2** What sort of magazine do you think would be the most interesting to work for?

**3** **You are going to listen to three people talking about their jobs working for a magazine. Match these words from the listening with their meanings.**

1 stuff

2 loads!

3 a buzz

4 a downside

5 a pain

a) a problem

b) a disadvantage

c) things

d) excitement

e) lots

**4** (34) **Look at the cards below. Listen and complete them.**

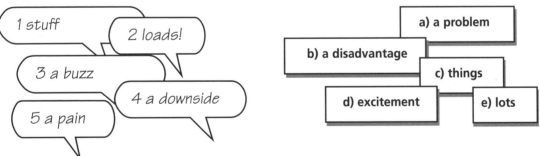

**First Speaker**

Name: ....................
Magazine: ....................
Job: ....................
Good points: ....................
....................
Bad points: ....................

**Second Speaker**

Name: ....................
Magazine: ....................
Job: ....................
Good points: ....................
....................
Bad points: ....................

**Third Speaker**

Name: ....................
Magazine: ....................
Job: ....................
Good points: ....................
....................
Bad points: ....................

**5** (34) **Listen again. Who talks about these things? Write G for Greta, H for Hope or J for James.**

1  a recipe ...................     3  make up ...........................     5  a covergirl ........................     7  manufacturers ...............

2  safety ......................     4  a diet ................................     6  Scotland...........................

**6** **Both Hope and James use the expression *I get to ... .*, e.g. *I get to keep some of the stuff I test. I get to interview racing drivers.* Tell your partner some things about yourself using this expression.**

Examples: *When my parents are out in the evening I get to watch what I want on TV.*
*When I go on holiday I get to stay up really late.*

**7** **Speaking. You and your partner have a paragraph about a person's job. There are some differences between them. Read your paragraph silently and then ask questions to find the differences. There are 20! Do not look at your partner's paragraph.**

**STUDENT A**
Wendy Masters is the night editor of a magazine. She's twenty-six years old and works for "Bananas" magazine in Marlwood. Her routine is unusual and quite different from a normal worker. She goes to work at 9 p.m. and gets home at 4 a.m.! When she gets home she doesn't go to bed immediately. She sits down and watches TV for half an hour with a hot drink to relax. Then she usually sleeps very well. Wendy wakes up at 12.30 p.m. and when everyone else has lunch she has breakfast! She likes toast and jam but she sometimes cooks bacon and eggs. She always has two cups of coffee to wake up. At about 2 p.m. she goes to the gym with her friend Lindsay and stays there for an hour. She usually walks there because it is near her home. She meets her boyfriend Mark when he finishes work and they sometimes eat out together. Their favourite restaurant is Maples, which serves Canadian food. Then it's time for Wendy to get ready for work again. She puts on her suit and drives her red Toyota to the magazine for another night.

YAWN!

**STUDENT B**
Wendy Marton is the night editor of a newspaper. She's twenty-nine years old and works for "The Morning News" paper in Marlwood. Her routine is unusual and quite different from a normal worker. She goes to work at 7 p.m. and gets home at 2 a.m.! When she gets home she doesn't go to bed immediately. She sits down and reads for half an hour with a glass of milk to relax. Then she usually sleeps very well. Wendy wakes up at 12.00 p.m. and when everyone else has lunch she has breakfast! She likes toast and honey but she sometimes cooks eggs and pancakes. She always has three cups of coffee to wake up. At about 2 p.m. she goes to the shopping centre with her friend Paul and stays there for an hour and a half. She usually walks there because it is near her home. She meets her boyfriend Pete when he finishes work and they sometimes eat out together. Their favourite restaurant is "Oaks", which serves English food. Then it's time for Wendy to get ready for work again. She puts on her suit and drives her blue Toyota to the "Morning News" building for another night.

**8** **Writing. Choose another magazine job and give a short presentation of it to the group.**

**Can-do checklist**

☐ **I can give a mini presentation.**
☐ **I can understand colloquial language.**
☐ **I can understand specific and general information.**
☐ **I can talk about routines.**

# 40 PAYBACK TIME?

**1** **Talk to a partner about these questions.**

1 What sort of questionnaires can you find in magazines?
2 Why do you think people like them?

**2** **There is a new phone line service where you can answer different personality quizzes on the phone. Here are some of them. What sort of questions do you think they will ask you?**

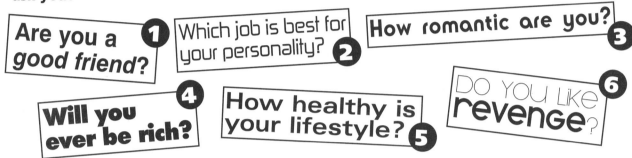

**1** Are you a good friend?
**2** Which job is best for your personality?
**3** How romantic are you?
**4** Will you ever be rich?
**5** How healthy is your lifestyle?
**6** Do you like revenge?

**3** 35 **Listen to a recorded message from a personality quiz phone line. Tick the above quizzes they mention.**

**4** **You are going to do a quiz about revenge. First match the words below to find three expressions of revenge and three of forgiveness. Write R or F beside each one.**

| | |
|---|---|
| 1 hold ◯ | a) the past behind you |
| 2 get ◯ | b) up |
| 3 put ◯ | c) back |
| 4 make ◯ | d) hands |
| 5 pay ◯ | e) a grudge |
| 6 shake ◯ | f) my own back |

**5** **Before you listen to the quiz, complete these sentences with the words below.**

argument   sensible   immature   go jump   dump   nasty

1 Her brother is so .............................. . He'll grow up soon I suppose!

2 I'm not speaking to her. We had an .............................. .

3 He's such a creep. I told him to .............................. .

4 Did you .............................. your girlfriend? I thought she was really cool.

5 My mum's .............................. . She always knows the right thing to do.

6 He said some really .............................. things about the teacher.

**6** 🎧 **Listen to the questionnaire and fill in the gaps.**

**1** After an ..................... how long have you been angry with someone?
**A** a few ..................... **B** a few days
**C** a few weeks **D** for ever

**2** Someone tells you that your boyfriend or girlfriend is going out with someone else in ..................... . What do you do?
**A** talk to him/her **B** dump him/her
**C** ..................... up his/her clothes **D** shout at him/her

**3** You plan a ..................... out with your friends. No one comes. What do you do?
**A** never speak to your friends again
**B** have a big .....................
**C** think "Oh well" and ask them out again.
**D** get angry but forget it tomorrow.

**4** A friend makes a ..................... about you. What do you do?
**A** laugh with everyone **B** talk to your friend later **C** shout at him/her in front of everyone
**D** never speak to him/her again.

**5** You meet your ..................... with his/her new partner. What do you do?
**A** leave **B** say hello
**C** give them a ..................... look **D** argue

**6** Your ex ..................... up with his/her new partner. Do you …
**A** feel sorry for him/her? **B** feel ..................... ?
**C** tell all your friends? **D** phone him/her to laugh about it

**7** Your ex wants to go out with you again. What do you do?
**A** ..................... and make up
**B** make up but be .....................
**C** tell him/her to go jump
**D** take some time to think about it.

**8** You go out with someone ..................... . Do you...
**A** tell the new person everything about your ex?
**B** ..................... why you broke up?
**C** keep talking about your ex?
**D** never talk about your ex?

**7** **Now answer the questions and calculate your score.**

**1 A** 1 **B** 2 **C** 3 **D** 4     **2 A** 1 **B** 3 **C** 4 **D** 2     **3 A** 4 **B** 2 **C** 1 **D** 3     **4 A** 1 **B** 2 **C** 3 **D** 4
**5 A** 2 **B** 1 **C** 3 **D** 4     **6 A** 1 **B** 2 **C** 3 **D** 4     **7 A** 1 **B** 2 **C** 4 **D** 3     **8 A** 4 **B** 3 **C** 2 **D** 1

**8** 🎧 **Listen to the analysis and answer these questions.**

**1** Do you agree with YOUR analysis?
**2** Which section mentions the following words? Use the key and write the correct numbers.
a = 28-32  b = 20-27  c = 10-19  d = under 10

**1** complain ☐     **2** centre ☐
**3** nasty ☐     **4** grudge ☐
**5** close ☐     **6** future ☐
**7** hurt ☐     **8** sensible ☐

**9** **Speaking. Here are some examples of paybacks. What do you think happened to make the people do these things?**

*I let his tyres down.*
*I threw her phone in the river.*
*I put salt in his coffee.*

**10** **Writing. With a partner choose another subject for a personality quiz from activity 2. Think of four situations with four choices for each situation. Then write a short analysis. Remember to use the present tense. Change partners and read your test to your new partner. Analyse him/her.**

**Can-do checklist**
☐ **I can use idioms.**
☐ **I can understand specific and general information.**
☐ **I can write a questionnaire/quiz.**
☐ **I can speak clearly.**

# VOCABULARY 2

**1** **Choose the correct word to complete these sentences.**

**1** We put some money .................. every month for a holiday.
A apart   B over   C aside

**2** I can't .................. a new car yet.
A earn   B afford   C spend

**3** He .................. all his money on CDs.
A paid   B spent   C put

**4** Are you .................. up for anything special?
A saving   B working   C earning

**5** When I was a child I got £5 .................. money a week.
A purse   B spend   C pocket

**2** **Reorder these words to make sentences.**

**1** off the I socks my supermarket at worked .................................................................................................

**2** grammar my in really English head does .................................................................................................

**3** have the you you to past behind put .................................................................................................

**4** putting am foot it my always in I .................................................................................................

**5** hurt back get he'll own him his but she .................................................................................................

**3** **Choose the correct words from the box to complete the sentences.**

**1** He's famous .................. his blond hairstyle.

**2** I'm fed .................. with exams!

**3** I'll pay you .................. for those terrible things you said.

**4** My grandfather ran .................. his neighbour's cat.

**5** The Beckhams had another argument but they'll make .................. soon.

**6** I can't walk .................. a chocolate shop!

**7** I'm going to throw .................. those old magazines. I don't need them now.

**8** The shop is always packed .................. on Saturday morning.

**9** Are you good .................. mending computers?

**10** Parents are always hard .................. their children.

> away
> on
> past
> at
> over
> back
> up
> for
> out
> up

**4** **Underline the correct word in the sentences.**

**1** I've got too much **things/stuff** in my bag.

**2** Don't talk to her – she's a real **pain/hurt**.

**3** There's a **downstairs/downside** to living with your parents.

**4** When I sing on stage it gives me a **buzz/a hum**.

**5** She bought a new **outsuit/outfit** for the wedding.

**6** Scissor Sisters played a **gig/gag** in Hyde Park.

**7** Can I try this on in the **moving/changing** rooms?

**8** The film is about a woman who wants **killing/revenge**.

**9** On the tongue we have loads of taste **buds/flowers**.

**10** This school has an excellent **reputation/result**.

**5** **Complete the adjectives in these sentences.**

1 He can do many things. He's **v** ☐☐☐☐☐☐☐☐☐ .

2 I can't stop playing this computer game. It's **a** ☐☐☐☐☐☐☐☐ .

3 She always says what she thinks. She's **o** ☐☐☐☐☐☐☐☐ .

4 I keep singing that song. It's **c** ☐☐☐☐☐☐ .

5 He loves to win. He's **c** ☐☐☐☐☐☐☐☐☐☐ .

6 That top is horrible! It's **g** ☐☐☐☐ .

7 There are many opinions for and against the idea. It's **c** ☐☐☐☐☐☐☐☐☐☐☐☐☐ .

8 It takes ages to do these puzzles. They're **t** ☐☐☐ **c** ☐☐☐☐☐☐☐☐ .

9 If you work hard and get a result it's **r** ☐☐☐☐☐☐☐☐ .

10 She writes wonderful stories. She's so **i** ☐☐☐☐☐☐☐☐☐☐ .

**6** **Unjumble the letters in capitals to find the verbs.**

1 Put your hands together. ................................... PLAC

2 To say a rhythmic poem. ................................... TANCH

3 To shout loudly. ................................... LELY

4 To shout when something good happens. ................................... RECEH

5 To get your money back in a shop. ................................... NERDFU

6 To finish with your partner. ................................... PUMD

7 To be embarrassed. ................................... GRICEN

8 A bomb does this. ................................... DOXPELE

**7** **Answer the clues to complete the crossword.**

**Clues across**
1 Tells you how to make a meal
5 Very good looking
6 When you go red
9 A very quiet person
11 A fire does this
12 It doesn't let in water

**Clues down**
2 On the front of a magazine
3 Strange person
4 Someone not invited to a party
7 Flashy jewellery
8 Knows what to do
10 Things

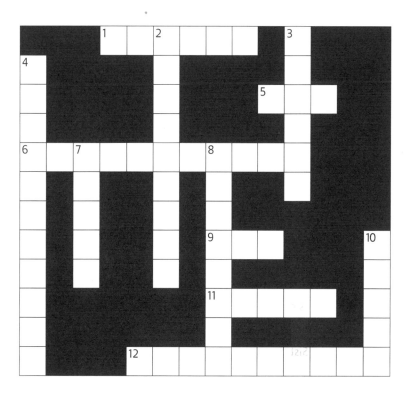

# TEST 4 LISTENING

## Part 1  Questions 1–6

138) There are seven questions in this part. For each questions there are three pictures and a short recording. Choose the correct picture and put a tick in the box below it.

**1**  Where is the partywear?

**2**  Who's playing?

**3**  Who is Jay's sister?

**4**  What happened at the party?

**5**  How did he die?

**6**  Who is she talking to?

## Part 2  Questions 7–12

You will hear someone talking about a famous person. For each question put a tick in the correct box.

**7** A  Everyone knows who David Acorah is. ☐
   B  Some people know him from TV. ☐
   C  Some people know him from the ☐
      newspapers and books.

**8** His job is
   A  a footballer. ☐
   B  someone who writes ghost stories. ☐
   C  someone who talks to ghosts. ☐

**9** When people say bad things
   A  he gets angry. ☐
   B  he doesn't care. ☐
   C  he argues with them. ☐

**10** Some people think
   A  the TV show doesn't show the truth. ☐
   B  the TV show is horrible. ☐
   C  the TV show is very frightening. ☐

**11** When David is talking to the writer
   A  he tells him some things about the past. ☐
   B  he tells him some things about the present. ☐
   C  he tells him some things about the future. ☐

**12** The writer
   A  thinks he's a fake. ☐
   B  isn't sure if he's a fake or not. ☐
   C  thinks he isn't a fake. ☐

## Part 3  Questions 13–21

You will hear a radio announcement. For each question fill in the information in the numbered boxes.

Name of Shop: (13) Designer ................................................

Date of opening: (14) ................................................

Sells clothes and (15) ................................................

Also has a (16) ................................................  to meet friends and

a (17) ................................................  for the children.

Discount of (18) ................................................

Free (19) ................................................

Time: (20) ................................................

Place: (21) Hightown's ................................................

## Part 4  Questions 22–27

Look at the six sentences for this part. You will hear a conversation between a boy called Gary and a girl called Sally about a party. Decide if each sentence is correct or incorrect. If it's correct, circle A. If it's incorrect, circle B.

**22** Sally is definitely not going to the party.   **A  B**

**23** Gary isn't worried about gatecrashers.   **A  B**

**24** Gary hopes there won't be too many people.   **A  B**

**25** Sally thinks it will be a great party.   **A  B**

**26** Gary's parents trust him.   **A  B**

**27** Sally worries a lot.   **A  B**

# TEACHER'S NOTES AND TRANSCRIPTS

## 1 WHO WANTS MY ...?

1 Lead in by giving an example of something you've recently bought that you don't like. Students work in pairs. Feedback interesting points from the conversations to the full group.
2 The students answer individually. Elicit and demonstrate the meaning of "swap".
3 Talk about the website. Let students predict in pairs.
4 **Key:** A 4  B 2  C 5  D 6  E 1  F 3
   Check against their predictions.
5 **Key:** 1 B  2 D  3 E  4 A  5 C  6 D & F  7 C  8 F
6 **Key:** car – blue  old   book – brand new   dress – black, small, designer   dictionary – heavy, enormous   CDs – old, valuable, fantastic   laptop – slow, heavy
7 Model sentences for the students to use in the task.
8 Allow time for the students to think and write down notes before the role play. Monitor and feedback interesting items/conversations to the group.
9 The students write the advertisement either in class or for homework. Copy them so that other students can read the adverts. Ask if anyone will swap!

## 2 IT'S ILLEGAL

1 Have a brief discussion about how much your students use computers. In pairs, students complete the puzzle.
   **Key:** 1 chatroom  2 e-mail  3 screen  4 click  5 server  6 surf  7 hacker
   Elicit and explain meaning of "hacker" – a computer expert who can get into any computer system illegally to access and change data.
2 Elicit predictions from the title.
3 **Key:** 1 C  2 C  3 B
4 **Key:** 1 A  2 B  3 B  4 B
   Explain the different words and present them in context.
5 Encourage a short discussion about such a high school in pairs followed by group feedback. (It is true!)
6 **Key:** 1 e  2 d  3 f  4 a  5 g  6 c  7 b
   Elicit connections with the pictures.
7 The students write the questionnaire in pairs. Feedback and check accuracy before the next stage.
   **Key:** 1 How often do you use a computer? 2 Which websites do you visit? 3 Do you prefer e-mailing or phoning? 4 Do you send/receive many e-mails? 5 Do you ever visit chatrooms? 6 Which server do you use? 7 Is your computer safe? 8 Do you get a lot of spam? 9 Do you have a firewall? 10 Do you have anti-virus software?
8 The students conduct the survey and record the results. Feedback and analyse results on the board.
9 This can be set as homework. It can be started 'Dear Editor ...'

## 3 THE LOVE OF YOUR LIFE

1 Lead in by eliciting words connected with dating. Students work in pairs to unscramble anagrams. You may need to explain some words.
   **Key:** 1 blind date  2 party  3 agency   4 personal ad  5 online  6 holiday  7 café
2 Students discuss in pairs and feedback interesting points.
3 It's a special test to find out what your future partner will be like. Ask students if they do magazine questionnaires about perfect partners and what they think of them.
4 **Key:** 1 hesitate  2 turning point  3 latest  4 techniques
5 **Key:** Place: Churchill Room  Hotel: Royal  Date: Tuesday 29th June  Times: 7.30-10.00 pm  Cost: free  Contact: Julie Simms
6 Students discuss what they think speed dating is. Explain more fully what happens at a speed dating session, i.e. only a few minutes to talk to each person to get an impression.

**Key:** B
7 Set the situation and give an example model. Elicit other questions that could be asked and put some on the board.
8 Check through the comment words and ask students to copy your pronunciation and intonation, e.g. BOR-ing! The students do the role play. If possible, arrange the group so that one set of students remain seated while the others rotate. One set of students, boys/girls, sits at a table. The second set (opposite sex) sit opposite. They have a short conversation and then after two minutes say "Change" and the second set of students move round to the next tables. Feedback on any interesting questions and responses.
9 The students write the e-mail in class or at home.

## 4 JUST FOR LAUGHS

1 If you know a simple joke, tell the students.
   **Key:** 1 practical joke  2 joke  3 hoax
2 The students talk about the questions with their partners. Feedback.
3 **Key:** A 1  B 3  C 2
4 **Key:** 1 false  2 crawl  3 melt  4 dye
5 **Key:** 1 C  2 B  3 A
   Elicit reasons for the choices.
6 **Key:** 1 put  2 played  3 crawled  4 used  5 thought  6 went  7 had  8 came  9 emptied  10 got  11 killed  12 left  13 looked  14 made  15 was
7 Model the expressions. The students listen and repeat. Tell the students some simple jokes and elicit reactions. They attempt to tell their partner a joke.
8 Look at the pictures with the students and check they have the necessary vocabulary.

## 5 CHOCOLATE

1 Ask students to close their eyes. Say the word "Chocolate" and ask them how it makes them feel. Ask students about their favourite sweets. In pairs, students find the words.
   **Key:** 1 late  2 cool  3 hat  4 tea  5 tool  6 chat  7 coach  8 hot  9 hate  10 tale
2 Students think of adjectives.
3 Check if they thought of any on the list.
   **Key:** colour – dark, milk, white  taste – sweet, silky, smooth, sickly  other – addictive, irresistible, fattening, moreish, tempting, messy
4 **Key:** A Chocolate of the night  B Obsession   C More
   Elicit different brands of chocolate. Ask why they are popular.
5 Students read and answer questions.
   **Key:** 1 C  2 B
6 Elicit further addictions.
7 The students match the collocations. Ask them to put the collocations in sentences.
   **Key:** addicted to     hooked on  give up   cut down   obsessed with
8 Check students can use the expressions. Monitor while they are doing the role plays. Discuss various pieces of advice afterwards.
9 The letter can be done for homework or completed in class.

## 6 WORK OUT

1 Lead in by asking the students how fit they are. Students discuss questions in pairs and feedback to the group.
2 Students do the wordsearch.
   **Key:** aerobics  squash  yoga  swim  tennis  weights  badminton  eat  drink  circuits  kick boxing  football
3 **Key:** You can do all of them.
4 **Key:** 1 Biggin Road  2 soft music  3 four types  4 four classes

5 Yes. Olympic size  6  four trainers   7 apple curry

5 **Key:** chef – Lionel   receptionist – Helen   swimming instructor – Sam   aerobics instructor – Kate   nursery nurse – Jodie   tennis coach – Kev   lifeguard – Tom   shop assistant – Petrina
Elicit the jobs and one sentence to say what each does.

6 Students discuss the questions in pairs and/or groups.

7 The students look at the situation. Explain it if necessary. Go through the expressions with the students and practise with different examples, e.g. "We should start with an aerobics class and then ...". Students work in pairs to plan the day. Feedback on any interesting points and elicit examples of making arrangements. Reinforce the expressions using examples from the students' plans.

8 The students write up the plan in class or at home.

## 7 TELLING WHOPPERS

1 Lead in by telling students to ask you a question to which you obviously lie in your answer,  e.g. Where are you from? Talk about how bad a lie it is. The students order the collocations.
**Key:** the truth   a fib   a white lie   a lie   a whopper

2 Encourage the students to talk about the questions in pairs and feedback to the group.

3 The students read the article quickly to answer the gist question.
**Key:** B

4 The students read again more slowly and work together to fill in the actions. Feedback and explain any unknown meanings. Model the verbs for pronunciation.
**Key:** 1 pupils get bigger   2 look left and down   3 scratch nose   4 smile   5 cross legs   6 tap toes   7 hesitate   8 sweat   9 touch ear   10 blush   11 lick lips   12 swallow

5 **Key:** 1 language   2 subject   3 giveaway   4 catch   5 sure

6 The students test each other.

7 **Key:** 1 FIBLUSH   2 CHEWHOPPER   3 SWEATAP
4 TRUTHESITATE   5  PUPILSCRATCH

8 Give some examples of your own to see if the students can tell if you're lying. They then write their own sentences to tell each other. Feedback.

9 Model the phrases for pronunciation practice before the students do the task. Put the phrases in context for them. e.g. *It's no problem if it's only a fib!*

10 The students can do the writing task in class or for homework.

## 8 THAT'S THE LIMIT

1 Lead in by asking the students if they drive – if not, why not – to elicit "age limit". The students do the word search.
**Key:** age   alcohol   speed   money   weight   height   time

2 The students scan the texts to match to the limits and guess the places.
**Key:** A age (shop)   B weight (airport)   C time (exam)
D height (theme park)   E money (cashpoint)
F speed (magazine)   G alcohol (advertisement)

3 **Key:** A too young   B too heavy   C too short   D too fast
Elicit other situations when these sentences could be said.

4 **Key:** 1 until – up to   2 further – more than
3 beneath – under   4 crashed – broke

5 **Key:** 1 16  2 18  3 16  4 18  5 18  6 17  7 17  8 18  9 18  10 21
*can* means – b possibility have. "It is possible to ..."

6 Contrast the limits in England and your country(ies). Model the sentences. Elicit the responses by saying some silly things and some sensible ones.  The students discuss the points and feedback to the group.

7 The students do the writing in class or at home. Give some examples first, e.g. you can travel in space at 7 years old.

## 9 PAGETURNERS

1 Lead in by asking the students about what they are reading at the moment (if anything) and why it's good or bad. Elicit the meaning of "pageturners".
**Key:** 1 An exciting book that you want to keep reading.

2 thriller, romance, detective, horror, sci-fi

2 **Key:** A romance   B thriller/detective

3 Tell students that some words may be appropriate to both.
**Key:** *Love in the Tropics* – lips, swimming, exciting, sunbed, relaxed, handsome, Gucci,   iced drink, heart, took off
*Deadly Nightshade* – blood, moonlight, shock, pale, dirt, fixed, violent, prison, dead, trees

4 Elicit what sort of beginnings the two books might have. Then students work in pairs to fill the gaps.
**Key:** *Deadly Nightshade:* 1 dead   2 fixed   3 shock
4 violent   5 blood   6 moonlight   7 trees   8 dirt   9 pale   10 prison     *Love in the Tropics:* 1 sunbed   2 iced drink   3 relaxed   4 Gucci   5 handsome   6 lips   7 exciting   8 swimming   9 heart   10 took off

5 A – 1 on her face   2 the night sky   3 Martha Tinsley
4 white     B – 1 by the pool   2 beside her   3 Gemma
4 swimming instructor

6 Go through the expressions with the students and practise pronunciation. Give some situations to allow them to respond.
Set up the task by giving the first sentence and changing one word. The students should stop you with an expression. They complete the activity in pairs.

7 Elicit some adjectives to describe books and put on the board. Students do the activity.
**Key:** Positive – clever, exciting, romantic, funny, unputdownable, informative  Negative – boring, disappointing, heavy, confusing  Either – scary, terrifying
Give an example of one book for each adjective, e.g. clever – Agatha Christie detective story.

8 Students discuss. Feedback interesting points to full group.

9 The students work in pairs to imagine and write an ending. Monitor and help as necessary. Copy or let students read their paragraphs to the class. Vote on the best.

## 10 THEME NIGHTS

1 Lead in by seeing how much your class know about England. Ask if they know the name of the Queen and the Prime Minister, and how many English cities they know. They then do the short quiz. Feedback.
**Key:** example answers – 1 Queen Elizabeth/Prince Charles/Prince William  2 Love Actually/Four weddings and a funeral/Notting Hill  3 Alice in Wonderland/Harry Potter/Jane Eyre  4 David Beckham/Tim Henman/Michael Owen
5 Mr. Bean/Wallace and Gromitt/Fawlty Towers
6 McFly/Oasis/Westlife

2 Students discuss. Feedback.

3 Students only look at the first paragraph.
**Key:** English Heroes and Heroines.
Elicit some examples.

4 Students read the rest of the text.
**Key:** James Bond  Harry Potter  Spice Girls  Queen Elizabeth  David Beckham  Dr Who  St. George

5 1 Dr Who  2 Harry Potter  3 Baby Spice  4 David Beckham
5 Queen Elizabeth  6 James Bond  7 St George

6 **Key:** 1 F  2 F  3 T  4 F  5 F

7 Elicit examples for heroes and heroines from your country. Put on board. Students then think of more. Feedback.

8 The students write the e-mail in class or at home.

9 The students do the information gap activity in pairs. Feedback.

## TEST 1 READING

1 B  2 C  3 B  4 A  5 C  6 E  7 C  8 B  9 A  10 D
11 B  12 B  13 A  14 A  15 B  16 A  17 B  18 B  19 B  20 B
21 B  22 D  23 B  24 A  25 D  26 C  27 B  28 A  29 B  30 D

## 11 DAVID WHO?

1 Lead in by putting an anagram of BECKHAM on the board. Say it's a famous English sports person and see who can guess it first. Ask students what they know about English football.

In groups, students think of international sports personalities.
**Key:** some suggestions – B: Boris Becker, Seve Ballesteros, George Best  E: Ernie Els, Jonathan Edwards  C: Jennifer Capriati  K: Kournikova, Kip Keino  H: Henri, Tim Henman, Padraig Harrington  A: Andre Agassi  M: John McEnroe

2 The students do the quiz.
**Key:** 1 a footballer  2 Real Madrid  3 Manchester United  4 Victoria  5 Singing with the Spice Girls  6 3  7 Brooklyn Romeo Cruz

3 The students match the collocations. Explain or elicit meaning.
**Key:** 1 score goals  2 greyhound racing  3 post box  4 cub camp  5 duck pond  6 football pitch

4 Explain that the Beckham Tour is a guided tour around the area where David Beckham lived as a child.
**Key:** 1 along  2 see  3 on  4 into  5 see  6 on  7 come  8 see  9 on  10 pass  11 past

5 **Tapescript**
*Welcome to the David Beckham tour. Please look at your map now. David Beckham was born on 2nd May 1975 at Whipps Cross hospital.  From here go north along Fullborne Road and turn left onto the North Circular Road. On the right you will see the Peter May Sports Centre.  Beckham played here for the under 10s and scored more than 100 goals in three years. Turn right into Chingford Mount Road and you will soon pass Walthamstow Stadium. David had a job here as a glass collector when there was greyhound racing and earned £10 a night. Carry on along Chingford Mount Road and turn right into Royston Avenue. You will come to Ainslie Wood. When David visited his grandparents who lived in the flats nearby he often played on the football pitches here. Go back and turn right into Chingford Mount Road then turn left into Hampton Road and second right into York Road. Here is David's first school – Chase Lane Junior School. Back to Chingford Mount again and turn right along Larkswood Road to Larkswood Park, David often played football here with his dad. Go north again along Old Church Road, over the crossroads and turn right into Nevin Drive. You will see Chingford School on your left, David's Secondary school. Go back to Old Church Road and turn right onto Mansfield Hill. Carry on along this road until you see the post box on your right. Turn right. You are now on Daws Hill. Carry on for about a mile. Go past a duck pond on the left and then on your right you will see the entrance to Gilwell Park – David was a cub scout and went on camp here. Obviously he went on to greater things!*
**Key:** 1 Whipps Cross Hospital  2 Peter May Sports Centre  3 Walthamstow Stadium  4 Ainslie Wood  5 Chase Lane Junior School  6 Larkswood Park  7 Chingford School  8 Gilwell Park

6 Students answer the questions in pairs before listening again.
7 Make sure students can give directions before doing the exercise.
8 Give students enough time to complete this exercise. It can be done at home.
9 If they can't be recorded, students can read them aloud.

## 12  I WANT TO BE A MILLIONAIRE

1 Lead in by asking students to name some popular TV quiz shows. They then discuss the questions in pairs and feedback.
2 Students do the multiple-choice task. Correct and elicit meanings of other words where appropriate. Give examples.
**Key:** 1 D  2 B  3 D  4 A  5 C  6 D  7 A
3 Before the students listen for the answers practise identifying long numbers. Say some numbers and the students write them down. Also check "How do you spell that?"
**Tapescript**
*Bart Damon: And here is our next contestant. So, Mr Simon Pritchard from Anglesea, are you ready to play for £2 million pounds?*
*Simon: I certainly am!*
*Bart: Just sit there. Right. Is that comfortable?*
*Simon: Yep.*
*Bart: So, Simon – how are you feeling at the moment?*
*Simon: Well – a bit hot and a bit nervous too …*
*Bart: Quite normal Si – can I call you Si?*
*Simon: Sure.*
*Bart: So, Si - are you usually good at quizzes?*

*Simon: I do quite a lot of quizzes and puzzles at home. I'm better with clues.*
*Bart: Well, no clues tonight I'm afraid.*
*Simon: I know!!*
*Bart: Now Si, just take some deep breaths and relax. It's going to be all right. So, Si, who have you brought with you tonight?*
*Simon: My wife, Anna. She's in the audience.*
*Bart: There's the lovely Anna. She's looking nervous too! And is there anyone watching at home?*
*Simon: My two kids – Matt and Katy. It's a bit late for them really, but it's a special occasion.*
*Bart: Yes, watching daddy win them lots of money.*
*Simon: I hope so!*
*Bart: And just how much money would you like to win tonight?*
*Simon: Well, as much as possible! Of course, I'd like to win the £2 million but really, £80,000 would be good.*
*Bart: And what would you do with that amount of money, Si?*
*Simon: I'd spend a lot of it on a holiday to America for the whole family and then I'd buy a car for my wife.*
*Bart: Lucky Anna!*
*Simon: And I'd buy a new car for me too! And of course some new toys for Matt and Katy. Maybe even a TV for the bedroom …*
*Bart: OK, OK!! Let's hope you win that money. Don't worry. Let's look at the first question. Remember you have …*
**Key:** 1 Simon Pritchard  2 Anglesea  3 Anna  4 Matt, Katy  5 £80,000  6 America  7 TV.

4 **Key:** 1 F  2 F  3 F  4 T
5 Tell the students what you would buy and then ask them to talk about it.
6 Do one example of a quiz question with multiple-choice answers before students do the task. Monitor and help.
7 The students practise the pronunciation of the phrases.
**Tapescript**

| | |
|---|---|
| *Is that comfortable?* | *Don't worry..* |
| *How are you feeling at the moment?* | *It's going to be all right.* |
| *Quite normal, Si.* | |
| *Can I call you Si?* | |
| *Just take some deep breaths. Relax.* | |

8 Give an easy example of the game with three simple questions to which they must remember the answers.
9 The students make up their own puzzles in class or for homework. Photocopy and distribute to the class.

## 13  BEST MATES

1 Lead in by asking what *mate* means. Ask if they can tell you about a famous TV show about a group of "mates" and name them. The students talk to each other about the questions.
2 Tell students that we often use some language in speech that we don't in writing. This is "colloquial". They match the formal and informal.
**Key:** 1 d  2 a  3 e  4 c  5 b
3 Tell the students to listen to the extract from the programme and ask some general questions, e.g. How many callers are there? Is the programme for younger or older listeners? The students work in pairs to unjumble the questions and then listen again to find the answers.
**Tapescript**
*Pam: If you've just joined us – you're listening to CoolFM and I'm Pam Parkes. We're having a phone in about best mates and what makes a good one! So, are you a good mate? And do you have any advice on how to be with your friends? Then phone in and tell me on air. The number is, as always, 098974581. And we have a caller on line 5. Hello line 5! Who am I speaking to?*
*Tracy: Hi. It's Tracy. Tracy Miles.*
*Pam: Good to talk to you, Tracy. And where are you from?*
*Tracy: Banner's Hill, near Markwood.*
*Pam: So, Tracy Miles from Banner's Hill, what do you want to say to our listeners?*
*Tracy: Yeah – well, I think the most important thing is to be straight up with your mates. You've always gotta be honest and tell them the truth.*
*Pam: I know what you mean.*
*Tracy: And you shouldn't ever, ever diss your best mate.*

*Pam: Yeah. Right. That is SO true. Sometimes I listen to people talking and I think "Duh? You're supposed to be best mates? I don't think so!"*

*Tracy: Yeh. And if someone else is dissing them, you've gotta speak up for them.*

*Pam: Wicked Tracy. Let's move on now to Line 7.*

*Jim: Hi Pam. I'm Jim from Browton ....*

*Pam: Jim, well – hello! You have a nice deep voice there!*

*Jim: Er – thanks.*

*Pam: And what have you got to say about mates?*

*Jim: I agree with Tracy. Also, I think it's really important to like your mates for who they really are. Don't try to change them.*

*Pam: That's why they're mates, isn't it? And Steve on Line 4. What makes a best mate a best mate Steve?*

*Steve: Well, Pam, it's all about being there for them. If your mate's down, you know got problems or feeling low, you've gotta listen to her and help her sort things out. That's the best sort of mate I think.*

*Pam: I think so too. And guys – if you've got mates like that – make sure you don't lose them! Now, some music ...*

**Key:** 1 What is the name of the radio station? CoolFM
2 What is the name of the presenter? Pam Parkes. 3 What is the phone in about? Best mates. 4 Who is the first caller? Tracy 5 What line is she on? Line five. 6 Where is she from? Banner's Hill. 7 Who is the second caller? Jim 8 What does the presenter like about him? He has a deep voice. 9 Who is the last caller? Steve.

4 The students do the matching task. Correct and then give further examples.
**Key:** 1 clicked 2 are into 3 hang out 4 stuff 5 left out 6 fancy

5 The students listen and repeat.
**Tapescript**
*Duh!*
*I don't think so!*
*That is so true!*
Give them other opportunities to practise these by giving different statements to which they respond.

6 Present the students with a problem, e.g. you're going to a wedding and you've got nothing to wear. Ask for advice and elicit some phrases. Then go through the expressions, practise pronunciation and put them in the context of your problem. The students do their own role plays. Feedback.

7 Ask students whether they read problem pages in magazines and get them to suggest types of problems. They can then choose one of these problems or one from activity 7 to write an answer to. This can be done in class or for homework. If the students are really interested they can all write a problem letter and exchange with another student for the reply.

8 The students can finally use the questions for a discussion on friends and family.

## 14 YOU ARE FEELING SLEEPY

1 Lead in by asking if anyone is tired and how the class slept last night. The students then work to unjumble the word. You can put this on the board and do as a class.
**Key:** Insomnia

2 In small groups students use the survey with each other. Ask them to record their answers and feedback.

3 **Key:** 1 read 2 bath 3 drink 4 exercise 5 sheep

4 This can be done in pairs or in full group.
**Key:** 1 B 2 C 3 B 4 A 5 B

5 Give students a couple of minutes to discuss and then write their ideas on the board.

6 Encourage the students to relax and to try not to laugh. They can cover their eyes with a form of blindfold to make the situation more realistic. The students don't think about any questions, they just relax and listen.
**Tapescript**
*First, make sure that you are comfortable. Is the room dark? Is it quiet? Good. Now, lie on your back with your arms beside you and close your eyes. Breathe in 2345678 and out 2345678. In ...out ...nice and easy, very slowly. Relax your muscles. Feel yourself getting more and more relaxed, your arms and your legs*

*are so heavy. The bed is like a cloud. You are sinking into it. In ... out ... in ... out ... . Now, I want you to imagine that you are in a lovely, old house. You are standing at the top of the stairs. From where you are standing you can see down, into the hall. The front door is open and outside you can see a beautiful garden in the sunshine. I want you to put your foot on the top step and now move slowly down to the next one. Can you still see the garden? There are ten steps and very slowly you are going to go down the stairs and across the hall to the garden. Look at the sunlight and the flowers. What sort of flowers are they? Down another step. Look through the flowers. There's a pond. The sun is shining on the water. You want to go outside. Down again. Think about the sunshine, how warm it will be on your skin. Down again. Another step and slowly another. You are nearly at the bottom. The lovely garden is nearer. You can feel the sun coming through the door. Down again. In ... out, in ... out ... . Down. And down and ...*

7 After the first listening the students open their eyes and work with a partner to complete the sentences from memory.
**Key:** 1 back 2 muscles 3 eyes 4 in; out 5 cloud 6 stairs 7 hall 8 foot top 9 water 10 bottom 11 nearer
The students listen again to check.

8 The students work in pairs to write the notes for a recording. Check vocabulary first.

9 The students can change partners and then relax each other with their visualisations.

10 Students can try the experiment on the same partner or change.

11 This can be done in pairs in class or individually at home.

## 15 YOU'VE GOT MAIL

1 Lead in by writing the word "mail" on the board. Ask students what it means and what types you can get. Refer them to the questions. They work in pairs and then feedback.

2 Play the listening once. Students do the matching exercises.
**Tapescript**
*1 Father: Angela? Angela? Where are you? Your mother and I are not happy. You promised to be home by midnight and it is now 1 o'clock. If you're not home in half an hour you will be grounded for the next fortnight. Do you understand?*

*2 Boy: Angie. Hi – how are things? Bit of a surprise huh? Been a few years. Well – I haven't phoned because – well there's a reason. You see – I had a bit of trouble – you know, with the police – (laughs) and no I didn't escape to South America or the Costa del Sol! But – see, well – I did a bit of stealing. I know, I know – stupid, stupid. But I'm finished with that now and it would be good to see you again – if you want to. Well, if you do want to, I'll get you a visiting permit (off) OK OK I'm finishing yeah, you too mate! Sorry, got to go – it's exercise time. Write to me c/o HMS Prison, Winchester. Cheers.*

*3 Mr Barker: This is a message for Angela Bradley from Mr Barker. We haven't seen you for a week Angela. Also, you didn't finish your last assignment. Unfortunately, if you do not attend classes immediately or contact us with a good reason, we shall have to ask you to leave the college. I hope to hear from you as soon as possible.*

*4 Saleswoman: I am contacting you on behalf of Vidaphone to tell you about our very special offer. If you send fifty or more text messages a month we will give you twenty extra completely FREE! YOUR pleasure is OUR pleasure at Vidaphone.*

*5 Boy: Ange. I think you probably know what this is about? (pause) Um – I really like you a lot – you know that – but- we're very different and we want different things. I think I need to be on my own for a while – so, sorry Ange, and I hope you meet someone better than me. If you need a friend, I'll always be there for you. Bye.*

**Key:** 1 A 2 B 3 E 4 D 5 C
Ask why the students made these choices.

3 **Key:** 1 A 2 A 3 B 4 A 5 A 6 B

4 **Key:** A2 B1 C4 D2 E5 F4 G1 H3 I2 J1

5 **Key and tapescript:**
*1 If you're not home in half an hour, you'll be grounded for the next fortnight.*
*2 If you do want to, I'll get you a visiting permit*
*3 If you do not attend classes immediately, we shall have to ask you to leave the college.*
*4 If you send fifty or more text messages a month, we will give you twenty extra completely free!*

**5** *If you need a friend, I'll always be there for you.*
Play it again so that students can check their answers.

**6 Key:** A4 – irritated  B2 – sorry for someone  C5 – angry  D1 – worried  E3 – indifferent

**7** The students put the expressions into the columns. Then play the expressions for the students to practise.
**Key:** worried – 3, 7  feel sorry for – 1, 9  angry – **2** indifferent – 4, 6, 8  irritated – 10, 5
Give some more situations for the students to respond to.

**Tapescript**

**1** *What a pity!*
**2** *That's IT!*
**3** *What shall we do?*
**4** *Whatever.*
**5** *He's a real pain!*
**6** *So what?*
**7** *Oh, no!*
**8** *It's nothing to do with me.*
**9** *Poor thing.*
**10** *I'm getting fed up.*

**8** Students practise the expressions with the correct intonation.

**9** The students work in pairs. They choose which message to reply to. Model one conversation for the students first. Choose one of the stronger students to be your partner.

**10** The students can write the reply message in class or at home.

## 16  THE BEST DAY OF YOUR LIFE?

**1** Lead in by asking the students what they think the title refers to. They then discuss the questions in pairs. Feedback.

**2** The students work in pairs or threes to do the wordsearch.
**Key:** church  priest  hair  dress  speech  guest  groom  veil  video  bridesmaid  cake  ring  gifts  buttonhole
Explain or elicit meanings.

**3** Play the listening for the students to do the task.

**Tapescript**

*1 Bride: It was going to be a wonderful day. Everything was going well. The weather was great. Brilliant sunshine! My hair looked good – the dress was brilliant – all the guests arrived. In church it was perfect – until we had to exchange rings and I put the ring on David's right hand, instead of his left! I don't know why – perhaps I was nervous and I was in a hurry – but I put it on the right finger but on the wrong hand and he couldn't get it off! It stuck! So, we finished the service and went outside for the photographs but David's finger got bigger and bigger and redder and redder! He was in a lot of pain. In the end we had to go to the hospital and we left all the guests at the hotel for the reception without us!*

*2 Bride: Our wedding day was perfect. There were no problems. Not one! Wonderful day – sunshine – 150 happy guests…We got the plane to Canada for our honeymoon and had a fantastic fortnight. It was only when we got back my mother told us that two days after the wedding 100 of the guests got really ill and a lot of them had to go to hospital! It was on the front page of the local newspaper! So they won't have happy memories of our wedding day, will they!*

*3 Bridegroom: I shall never forget our wedding reception. My bride disappeared for two hours because her favourite pop star was signing copies of his new book at the local bookshop and she wanted to meet him! She didn't tell me she was going and I thought she'd left me an hour after the wedding!*

*4 Bridegroom: It was after the wedding that things went wrong for us. We got divorced seven months later! The sad thing was – we'd had this brilliant idea of making a video of the wedding. Not your normal video with everyone smiling and eating and dancing etc. but we made a pop video!! There's this special company that arrange it. They direct it and film it. We chose the song and practised our moves and miming to the words – we didn't really have to sing thank goodness!. The guests didn't know about it until they arrived at the church, then they joined in. Some people thought it was a bit strange – but – well, it was something different, wasn't it? It went so well – even the priest took part, and everyone was dancing in the church!! What is so sad is – the song we used was my favourite. But now, after the divorce, I think we should have chosen something different. It was the Bee Gees singing "Tragedy."!!*

**Key:** 1 D  2 C  3 A  4 B

**4** Play again. Students tick the words they hear.
**Key:** hair  dress  guest  church  ring  bride  video  priest

**5 Key:** 1 very bright sun  2 couldn't move  3 party after the wedding  4 moving your lips to a song.

**6 Key:** 1 B  2 A  3 C  4 B  5 A

**7** Tell the students that *get* is often used in spoken English instead of another verb. Elicit as many uses of *get* from the students as possible before doing the task.
**Key:** took (transport)  returned  finished a marriage  remove  increased  became

**8** Elicit more wedding day vocabulary onto the board. The students plan the catastrophe in pairs.

**9** They write the article in class or at home.

## 17  JUST THE JOB

**1** Lead in by asking the students if they are looking forward to starting work or if they enjoy being at school and why. The students discuss questions in pairs or small groups. Feedback.

**2** Elicit what the students think is important in a future job. Put suggestions on the board. The students do the crossword.
**Key:** 1 holiday  2 hours  3 promotion  4 manager  5 money  6 easy  7 inside
1 DOORMAN – gives security at entrance to clubs etc.
2 a bouncer  a door superviser
3 a night club  a pub  a hotel  a casino  a concert
4 a person who likes a job with people, a little different, exciting, unusual
5 someone who is good with people, with good discipline skills

**3** Play the recording.
**Key:** First speaker – A  Second speaker – B

**Tapescript**

*1 Man: Well, they're just criminals themselves, aren't they? Big, bald men who like fighting. It's just an excuse. An excuse for a fight. Not very intelligent either, if you ask me. Not much upstairs if you know what I mean. You see them outside the pubs and clubs walking around in their long, dark coats like they were the boss of the streets! More like the Mafia! Ooh – I wouldn't like to meet one of them on a dark night! Probably can't get any other job. Probably on drugs and things too. Terrible people, terrible!*

*2 Woman: A lot of my friends are door supervisors – men and women, and they're really nice people. Most people think door supervisors are big, beefy men who like fighting but that's not true. A good door supervisor doesn't fight unless he/she really has to. They have a special licence and they're trained to talk to people who cause trouble so that there aren't any fights. They have to be diplomatic and polite. The best door supervisor I know is a tiny woman! She's brilliant. To be a door supervisor isn't easy. They have to pass exams and of course, the job can be dangerous. The hours aren't good – always late nights. But people who become door supervisors are usually very sociable – they like other people, and they like doing something a bit different – not the normal 9-5 job. The job's freelance – you work for yourself and the pay's pretty good too but it's only part time and a lot of door supervisors have a day job too. So you can be a door supervisor at night and a business executive during the day!*

**4 Key:** 1 A  2 A  3 B  4 B  5 A 6 B  7 B  8 A

**5 Key:** 1 bald  2 tiny  3 sociable  4 diplomatic  5 beefy  6 free lance  7 part time

**6** The students write the questions and then practise with the jobs given, e.g. "How many days holiday does a hairdresser have?" "I'm not sure. Probably a few weeks." Put some examples on the board.

**7** Give the students a model. Choose a job yourself and get them to ask you some questions. The students then work in pairs. They can choose one of the jobs from the previous exercise or something completely different. If a student is struggling, his/her partner can give clues.

**8** The students prepare a mini presentation based on what they have previously discussed/practised, using notes. Give a short example of your own to help them. Put useful expressions on the board, e.g. "This is a good job because …"

**9** Students write up the presentation in class or at home.

## 18 NO ONE HERE BUT US ROBOTS

**1** Lead in by eliciting the meaning of "automated". Write the word on the board and ask for ideas. Elicit types of automation, e.g. ticket machines at stations, etc. Ask students for a word they can make from it, e.g. *mate*. Students then work together to see how many they can find. Feedback.

**2** Students discuss the questions.

**3** Elicit any vocabulary from the pictures.

**Tapescript**

*1 On the third stroke it will be …*

*2 … going to receive some important news about money. Be brave and …*

*3 … you are looking for is 01861 3346123 …*

*4 ….cold in the north and very rainy. In the south there will be a lot of sunshine throughout the day but in the evening it…..*

*5 ….is blocked because of an accident. There is a five mile traffic jam so motorists are advised to take…..*

*6 … see a doctor if it doesn't get any better in twenty-four hours …*

**Key:** 3, 4, 5, 1, 6, 2

**4** Talk about this question with the full group.

**5** Play the recording.

**Key:** It's a fun recording. Reasons – the interruptions and type of language the recording uses.

**Tapescript**

*A: You have reached the automated ticket line for IKON cinemas. Where would you like to see a film?*

*B: In the cinema.*

*A: Perhaps you didn't understand. Which town would you like?*

*B: Nottingham.*

*A: Please wait. Beep beep beep….. This is the ticket line for Ikon cinemas in Notting Hill.*

*B: No. Not Notting Hill! Nottingham.*

*A: Sorry. This is the ticket line for HAMpton.*

*B: Nottingham. Nottingham. You know – Robin Hood*

*A: Thank you. This is the ticketline for Nottingham. Which film would you like to see? "Harry Potter and the Temple of Doom" "Lord of the earrings" "Friday 13th, Friday 14th, Friday 15th, Friday 16th"*

*B: Yes Friday the…*

*A: Wait! Let me finish the list.*

*B: Sorry.*

*A: Thank you. "Toy Dogs" "Draculina" or "The Phantom of the Opera."*

*B: Friday 13th.*

*A: Yes?*

*B: Please.*

*A: Certainly. Which date?*

*B: Friday 18th please.*

*A: Thank you. Which showing? 2.00 or 3.15.*

*B: 3.15*

*A: Ah ah 4.00, 4.45, 5.30 or 6.00?*

*B: 3.15……. Please.*

*A: And how many tickets would you like?*

*B: Two… Please.*

*A: And your credit card number?*

*B: 96871540923*

*A: Good. Almost there. You have booked 22 tickets for Phantom of the Opera at 12.15 on Friday 13th. Thank you.*

*B: What? But that's…*

*A: Thank you.*

*B: But I didn't*

*A: Sorry. This is a bad line. Goodbye. Please use this ticketline again. Beep!*

**6** Play the recording again.

**Key:** 1 A  2 C  3 B  4 C

**7 Key:** Phantom of the opera  Friday 13th  12.15  22 tickets. Friday 13th  Friday 18th  3.15  2 tickets

**8 Key:** 1, 4, 5, 8, 11

1 P  2 M  3 P  4 C  5 P  6 B  7 P  8 P  9 B  10 M  11 M  12 M

**9** Give an example of your own to model for the students, e.g. "Put two eggs and some butter into the …"  The students then work in pairs.

**10** This gives students practice saying phone numbers.

**11** Students work together to create a longer message. They can choose one of the subjects given in the unit or something else. If possible record some of the messages after checking.

## 19 WHAT'S THE GOSS?

**1** Lead in by asking the students what "goss" is short for (gossip). Students discuss questions in pairs or small groups.

**2 Key:** skinny – thin  hunky – handsome  oldies – parents  an item – a couple  to dump – to finish with  to wind up – to joke with  fortnight – two weeks

**3** Play the recording. Students match to the pictures.

**Tapescript**

*1 A: Hi! It's me. You're never going to believe this but guess who I saw at the supermarket today?*

*B: Well, go on. Tell me.*

*A: Miss Dean.*

*B: So? She's allowed to go shopping.*

*A: But she was with someone …*

*B: Probably her fiancé – you know she's engaged.*

*A: But it wasn't him!*

*B: Come on – you know you're bursting to tell me.*

*A: Miss Dean was holding hands with Mr. Munroe by the baked beans.*

*B: Not that creepy guy from the Maths department with thick specs and spots?*

*A: The same!*

*B: That's great news.*

*A: Why?*

*B: That means her hunky fiancé is single again!*

*2 A: Hi! It's me again. Don't faint but did you know that your ex – Dave – has become a male model?*

*B: Dave! You're having a laugh.*

*A: I kid you not! He's in this week's "Man" magazine – on the cover!*

*B: But he was such a skinny little guy.*

*A: Well he looks fit, rich and he's got his arm round Britney Spears.*

*B: And to think I dumped him!*

*A: That's life!*

*3 A: Hi! What about Becky Parks then?*

*B: What about her?*

*A: Don't tell me you don't know?*

*B: What is it that I don't know?*

*A: She's had a nose job!*

*B: Never!*

*A: That's why she's been off school for a fortnight.*

*B: But I thought she was on holiday with the oldies.*

*A: That was the idea. She didn't want anyone to know.*

*B: So, how do you know?*

*A: Well, her brother told Mike and Mike told his mum, then his mum told my mum and I heard my mum telling my dad.*

*B: So, how does her nose look now?*

*A: Like a ski jump!*

*4 A: Hi, Jenny! Have you heard about Bob and Sandy?*

*B: Yeah. They're an item.*

*A: No, not that.*

*B: What then?*

*A: They got arrested last night.*

*B: NO.*

*A: They spent the night at the police station.*

*B: NO.*

*A: All they had to eat was dry bread and water.*

*B: You're joking.*

*A: Nope.*

*B: But why?*

*A: They were in a stolen car.*

*B: A stolen car?*

*A: It was used in a bank robbery.*

*B: A bank robbery?*

*A: And there was blood in the car.*

*B: Blood?*

*A: Yes – all over the seats.*

*B: You're winding me up.*

*A: Yep! It's so funny to see your reactions!!*

**Key:** 1 B  2 D  3 A  4 C

**4 Key:** 1 believe  2 guess  3 know  4 about  5 tell  6 heard  7 on  8 on  9 bursting  10 laugh  11 joking  12 winding  13 No

**5** Elicit answers from students.
**Key:** She says "NO" and she repeats words, e.g. "Blood?"

**6** Play the last conversation again. Students take Jenny's part.

**7** Students practise the correct intonation in new situations.

**8** Check vocabulary from the situations. Model one with a strong student. The students role play the situations.

**9** The students work with a sheet of paper to have a written conversation. They must not say a word.

## 20  DON'T SHOOT THE MESSENGER

**1** Lead in by leaving a message on the board for the students. Students discuss the questions in 1. Feedback.

**2** Give a model. Tell the students about an arrangement (e.g. for end of term party) and they note down important points. Then play the first conversation. Feedback main points.

**Tapescript**

*Terry: Hi! Can I speak to Jackie please.*
*Sue: Sorry. She's out at the moment. Can I give her a message?*
*Terry: Yeah. Could you tell her Terry called?*
*Sue: Right – Terry. (as if writing)*
*Terry: Yep. Tell her we're meeting in the car park at 4.30.*
*Susie: Car park. 4.30.*
*Terry: Ah ha. We're going in Owen's car. Tell her Marie can't come but Janet can.*
*Susie: Owen's car. Marie no but Janet yes.*
*Terry: We've booked a hotel for two nights and it's £25 each.*
*Susie: Hotel 2 nights. £25.*
*Terry: Yeah. Oh and can you ask her to bring her blue dress. We're going to a posh restaurant.*
*Susie: Blue dress. Is that it?*
*Terry: Yep. Thanks.*
*Susie: Do you want her to phone you back?*
*Terry: No. That's OK. I'll see her there.*

**3** Play second conversation. Students change details. Feedback.

**Tapescript**

*Terry: Hi! It's me, Terry, again. Is Jackie in yet?*
*Susie: Sorry. She's still out.*
*Terry: I've got a few changes in the message?*
*Susie: OK, go ahead.*
*Terry: Well, it's now 4 o'clock at the car park and we're taking Pete's car. There aren't enough seats in Owen's. And Janet can't come but Marie can.*
*Susie: 4 not 4.30. Pete's car not Owen's. Marie but not Janet.*
*Terry: And I got the price wrong. The hotel's £35 each.*
*Susie: £35.*
*Terry: We can't get a table at the posh restaurant so it'll be MacDonald's. She won't need the blue dress. OK?*
*Susie: No blue dress.*
*Terry: Thanks a lot!*

**4** Play third conversation. Students change details.

**Tapescript**

*Terry: It's me.*
*Susie: She's still out. Not more changes?*
*Terry: Sorry about this. Last ones. I promise!*
*Susie (sighs): All right. Shoot.*
*Terry: 4 o'clock at the station. We're getting the train. Pete's car has broken down. No Marie or Janet. Only one night at the hotel - they're overbooked. Posh meal is on again – someone cancelled so ...*
*Susie: Bring the blue dress?*
*Terry: Yep. Cheers!*

**5** Play final conversation.

**Tapescript**

*Terry: It's me. You're going to kill me. It's all off. Owen's ill. Pete's got no money. The train's too expensive and my parents want me to look after the dog for the weekend. Sorry!!*

**6** Play the recording again for students to answer the questions.
**Key:** 1 There are not enough seats.   2 They are going to a posh restaurant. 3 They can't get a table.   4 It's overbooked. 5 His car's broken down.   6 Someone cancelled.   7 Owen's ill Pete's got no money, the train's expensive and Terry has to look after the dog.

Check vocabulary from this exercise and test, e.g. The car

won't move = It's broken down, etc.

**7 Key:** Terry – 1 3 5 8   Susie – 2 4 6 7 9

**8** As in instructions on the students' page. Every other student has a text and reads it to the person on his/her right. This person notes down the important points. They then reconstruct the messages from the notes to give to the person on their right with two changes. This continues until all messages have been passed on. Compare final versions with the originals. The students must not see each other's texts. Before they do the task, pre-teach any necessary vocabulary.

**9** The students choose a message to write from the list. Model one first. "Your mum called to tell you that ..." The students write the messages in class or at home.

## VOCABULARY 1

**1** 1 out  2 up  3 with  4 for  5 away  6 to  7 to  8 up

**2** front door   football pitch   free lance   practical joke tennis court

**3** 1 My mother always taught me to tell the truth.
2 I can nearly remember it. It's on the tip of my tongue.
3 The police stopped me because I broke the speed limit.
4 When he's hungry he often licks his lips.
5 I don't like leaving voice mail. I never know what to say.
6 I had a virus on my computer and I lost a lot of my work.
7 She phoned the company but only got an automated message.
8 My friends met at a speed dating evening.

**4** 1 Jack and Jill have been <u>an item</u> for six months.
2 You must eat more. You're so <u>skinny</u>.
3 Have you seen that <u>hunky</u> guy who lives next door?
4 Please take your <u>stuff</u> off the table.
5 He <u>dumped</u> her when he saw her with his best mate.

**5** 1 hesitate  2 designer  3 violent  4 hack  5 fortnight 6 grounded

**6** 1 reception  2 dye  3 crawl  4 suspicious  5 illegal  6 outfit 7 height  8 assignment  9 diplomatic  10 insomnia  11 gossip 12 tiny  13 melt  14 win  15 bald

**7** Across: 1 swallow  5 defend  8 obsessed  12 spam  13 thriller 14 stairs  Down: 2 lie  3 fed  4 bride  6 fib  7 height  9 screen 10 swap  11 weight

## TEST 2 LISTENING

*Play each part twice.*

1 B  2 A  3C  4 C  5 B  6 C  7 B  8 C  9 B  10 B  11 A  12 C
13 Eva  14 Ben  15 the party  16 go to Glasgow  17 The Two Cats restaurant  18 the theatre  19 The Hilton Hotel  20 plane
21 tomorrow  22 A  23 B  24 B  25 B  26 B

**Tapescript**

*Part 1*

*1 Go along the High Street. Turn right at the garage into Long Road and it's on your left.*
*2 Ken: Do you ever do any puzzles?*
*Pat: Yeah. I usually do the Crossword at the back of the paper.*
*Ken: Have you tried those wordsearches or number games?*
*Pat: They're a bit boring.*
*3 Tina: I can never talk to my mum about big problems – she's too busy.*
*Linda: Have you ever written to a problem page?*
*Tina: No! I just tell you!*
*4 You're standing at an open door. You can see a river with a bridge. The sun is shining on the water.*
*5 It's Bill! Haven't heard from you for ages – since we left school! Well, YOU left school – I'm still there – the other end of the classroom! Are you still working at the gym? Give me a ring.*
*6 It was a disaster! One of the guests spilled red wine on my dress and the waiter dropped the cake on the floor!*

*Part 2*

*Hi! I'm John Parker with your weekly update on what's new on our TVs at the moment. It's been a pretty good week with a couple of excellent programmes on Channels 1 and 4.*
*On Friday we had the first in a new quiz show called "Happy Families". The contestants are all members of the same family playing against each other*

*for a big prize. The questions are quite difficult and not like your normal quiz show. They're interesting too – and if, like me, you play along at home – it could be quite an addictive series! Unfortunately the new series of "Wedding Bells" was boring, boring, boring! They say it's "new" but I'm sure we've all seen the video clips before – you know, the cake on the floor, the bride on the floor, the bridesmaids on the floor, the bride's mother on the floor!!*
*A programme I DID like was the gossip chat show on 4 called "What's the Story". There are talks with famous people but what's fun is that the people tell stories about themselves and others and the audience decides if they're telling the truth or lies! It was very funny. Watch it next week.*
*Well, that's it for this week – same time next week we'll have some opinions on the new thriller starting on Channel 3 next Saturday. Have a good week.*

### Part 3

*Hello. This is a message for Eva from Ben. Sorry I've missed you. You have probably left for tennis. I'm phoning to say that I'm really sorry but I can't come to the party tonight. I know I said I could but I've got to go to Glasgow for a really important football match. It's a college thing. They only told me last night – Tim's broken his leg and can't play – and it was too late to phone you then. We've got two matches and then we're having this special dinner at "The Two Cats" restaurant – very expensive! After dinner we're going to a show! I would really prefer to be at the party – but this is a real chance. I'm staying at the Hilton too – that will be fun! We're catching the plane to Glasgow at 10.30 so I have to go. I'll phone you tomorrow. Sorry again about this evening.*

### Part 4

*Debbie: So Sam, what are you doing next year? Are you applying for Uni?*
*Sam: Yeah. I'm going to try. I want to study sports science.*
*Debbie: Mmm. I think you'd be really good at that.*
*Sam: How about you Debbie?*
*Debbie: No. University's not for me. I've had enough of studying and teachers and school! I just want to get out into the world.*
*Sam: But you're going to get great results in your exams.*
*Debbie: I don't know. I want to do something different!*
*Sam: You can get a much better job with good money if you go to uni.*
*Debbie: Money's not everything Sam!*
*Sam: Life is better with money than without it!*
*Debbie: I want to travel. I want different things to you Sam.*
*Sam: I bet your parents don't like your plans.*
*Debbie: They don't know yet. And don't YOU tell them either Sam! I'm waiting for the right moment.*

## 21 WRITE ON!

1 Lead in by asking students if they can give one adjective to describe their personalities (or their partners). Look at the words in the box and ensure students can pronounce them. Students complete the crossword in pairs. The words may need more explanation. Elicit the meaning of "graphology".
**Key:** 1 outgoing 2 artistic 3 versatile 4 optimistic 5 enthusiastic 6 competitive 7 lively 8 outspoken 9 imaginative 10 shy
**Mystery word:** graphology.

2 Students ask their partners (and write down) which words they think describe themselves.

3 Ask students how much writing they do and what their handwriting is like. Students read and match.
**Key:** 1 large 2 small 3 tidy 4 untidy 5 slant to right 6 upright 7 high upper strokes 8 heavy pressure 9 light pressure 10 rounded letters

4 **Key:** c and d

5 Students talk about their impressions from the handwriting.

6 Students read to match the texts with the handwriting.
**Key:** 1 C 2 A 3 B

7 **Key:** 1 C 2 A 3 B

8 Students talk about these questions together or in full group.

9 Students do the writing task in class.

10 Students exchange paragraphs and analyse each other's writing. Remind them to look back at how each described his/her personality at the beginning. Feedback and check what the rest of the class thinks.

## 22 THE LATEST CRAZE

1 Lead in by looking at the title of the unit and elicit the meaning for "craze". Students look at options and choose.
**Key:** b

2 Using the pictures, elicit the crazes. Tell students about a craze from your childhood and talk about the questions.

3 Students match the adjectives to the pictures. Elicit other things the adjectives can describe to consolidate meaning.
**Key:** A maddening B time-consuming C rewarding D addictive

4 Students scan the article for the information.
**Key:** 1780 – the first idea for Sudoku 1980s – became popular in the USA 1984 – Developed in Japan 2004 – first appeared in a UK newspaper 1,000,000 – people play it every day 10 years – will it still be popular?

5 Students can read the article again to answer the questions.
**Key:** 1 F 2 F 3 F 4 T 5 T 6 T 7 F 8 T 9 F

6 Students read to fill the blanks.
**Key:** 1 grid 2 bold outline 3 row 4 smaller box 5 digit 6 column

7 Students try to do the puzzle using the expressions.

8 Students match and discuss in pairs. Feedback and ask students to explain puzzles.

9 Students write their own puzzles together. Monitor and help. Pairs exchange.

## 23 THE FAT DUCK

1 Ask students the first question. List answers on the board.
**Key:** b

2 Students read only the first sentence to check.

3 Before reading further students match the words and meanings.
**Key:** 1 reputation 2 syrup 3 combination 4 taste buds 5 motivate 6 recipe 7 explode
Clarify meanings and ask for/give context sentences.

4 Students read the article and do the task.
**Key:** 1 B 2 C 3 B 4 A 5 A

5 Students work out the questions and answers in pairs.
**Key:** 1 Q: What is the Fat Duck? A: A good restaurant
2 Q: What title did it win? A: Best restaurant in the world.
3 Q: Who owns the restaurant? A: Heston Blumenthal
6 Q: Why is it famous? A: Because of its strange combinations of flavours. 5 Q: Why does one dessert use nitrogen? A: To freeze the outside of the dessert. 6 Q: How much does a meal for two cost? A: A couple of hundred pounds
Ask students if it's possible to have a restaurant that is "best" in the world.

6 Students match the collocations. Feed back onto the board and ask students to provide other sentences or contexts to use them.
**Key:** famous for well known title goes to results are out latest search

7 Students should try to see what they can remember without looking back.
**Key:** 1 some of our foreign friends 2 than fish and chips 3 explodes on your tongue 4 to motivate their students 5 adventure for your taste buds

8 Students discuss the questions in pairs. Feedback interesting points to the full group. Put any new lexis on the board.

9 Set up the paired speaking task. Check that students understand all the words and stress this should be a discussion not simply "I think this" and "I think this". Go through the expressions, checking pronunciation and giving models. Give them several minutes for the discussion and then feedback.

10 Encourage the students to be creative. The restaurant can be "traditional" or "modern". If time and ability allows, they can go on to think about decoration, etc. Feedback and vote on the best ideas.

## 24 MONEY IN YOUR POCKET

1 Use the first question as a lead in.
   **Key:** c
2 Students discuss the questions in pairs and feedback.
3 Students read the chatroom conversation quickly to find the answers.
   **Key:** 1 Carly  2 £190 a month  3 11  4 Tim
   Ask for opinions on what the girls say in the conversation.
4 **Key:** 1 C  2 A  3 B  4 A  5 D  6 C  7 A
5 **Key:** 1 chore  2 work your socks off  3 spoilt  4 comics
6 This exercise tests vocabulary from the previous two exercises.
   **Key:** spend money on  put money aside  save up for  can't afford  keep tidy  work your socks off  do chores  earn money
   Personalise these expressions by asking students for sentences about themselves, e.g. "Is there anything you want but can't afford?" "I want a new computer but I can't afford it." Students can test each other by giving the first part of a collocation and their partner must give the other part.
7 Tell students that they are going to have a chatroom conversation. They write but must not open their mouths! Go through the expressions for opinion giving, saying they can be used both in speech and in writing.
8 Check that students have a sheet of paper for each pair and that they understand the task. Put the question on the board. Go through the ideas. Encourage students to focus on what they are writing about and not to be too concerned about accuracy at this stage. When they have finished they can spend some time checking accuracy. Feedback and continue the discussion orally. Put their ideas on the board and students can write up the discussion at home.

## 25 THE BEAUTIFUL PEOPLE

1 Lead in by eliciting some words that the students know meaning *beautiful*. They then find words in the wordsnake.
   **Key:** pretty  handsome  goodlooking  gorgeous  stunning  beautiful  lovely  ravishing  striking
   You can extend this by discussing opposites, e.g. ugly, etc.
2 Students discuss the questions in pairs and feedback.
3 Students read to check their answer.
   **Key:** online dating
   You may need to clarify this. Explain the meaning of "controversial".
4 Students read the article and do the task.
   **Key:** details should include  Mark: big nose/crooked teeth/scar/different eye colours    Jenny: lovely eyes/long, dark hair/perfect teeth/slim figure
5 **Key:** 1 F  2 T  3 F  4 F  5 F  6 T
   Ask students how they think Jenny really feels.
   **Key:** upset
6 Make sure that students know the meanings of the verbs by giving examples.
   **Key:** 1 definition  2 arrangement  3 application  4 acceptance  5 refusal  6 adoration
   Ask students to choose two verbs and write one sentence for each verb and one sentence for each noun to show how the words are used. Feedback.
7 Students work together in pairs to suggest the different things. Feedback and put examples on the board.
8 Students discuss the questions. Write answers on the board.
9 Students write the applications in class or at home. If in class, they can read the descriptions without giving the name and the class have to guess the beautiful person.

## 26 I'M HAVING A BAD DAY

1 Lead in by asking students about what they do before an exam – work/sleep/eat, etc. Students complete the crossword.
   **Key:** 1 cram  2 test  3 nervous  4 resit  5 stress  6 fail  7 forget  8 questions
   **Mystery word:** revision
2 Students think about what can affect their exam day. Feedback to the group.

**Key:** (examples) no sleep, get up late, bad weather, etc.
3 Students read quickly to identify subject.
   **Key:** B
4 Students read again to answer questions.
   **Key:** 1 C  2 A  3 A  4 A
   Ask students their opinions on what Lynne has written.
5 Elicit some excuses for being late/not giving in homework. Students read the excuse on the website and order the pictures.
   **Key:** 15%
6 Look at the phrases and check the pronunciation and meaning. Go through the example excuses. In pairs, students invent some good excuses, using some of the expressions and be more than one sentence.
7 Students write the excuses down and read them to the class – with a straight face!.

## 27 PARDON?!

1 Lead in by asking the students if they know any modern expressions in English, e.g. for describing some music they really like (cool). Students match the expressions. Emphasise that older age groups don't use the same words.
   **Key:** 1 well (it's well good)  2 gross  3 fit  4 bling  5 6 7 cool  wicked bad  8 sad
2 Students discuss the questions in pairs and feedback.
3 Elicit what the students think they might find on the website. They then read to answer the question.
   **Key:** No
4 The students look at the words and guess the meanings. Feedback interesting ideas!
   **Key:** -er and -an can indicate "a person."
5 The students read to match the words to the descriptions.
   **Key:** 1 shopgrifter  2 flexitarian  3 twixter  4 freegan
   Ask students if they know any people like this.
6 Students match the words to the pictures.
   **Key:** A freegan  B shopgrifter  C twixter  D flexitarian
7 Students can read again to answer the questions.
   **Key:** 1 B  2 C  3 A  4 C
8 **Key:** 1 return  2 suits  3 rent  4 protect  5 refund  6 waste  7 throw
9 The students work in pairs to try to guess the meanings. First check that they understand the clues. Feedback ideas.
10 Students make up their own words. Feedback onto the board. Other students have to guess what the new words mean.
11 Students write the dictionary definitions in class or at home.

## 28 CHEERS!

1 Lead in by eliciting meaning of "Cheerleading". Brainstorm what the students associate with this.
2 Students do the quiz in pairs.
   **Key:** 1 B  2 C  3 C  4 C  5 B  6 A  7 C
   Clarify meanings of any unfamiliar words, e.g. fit, flexible, pom poms, etc.
3 Students read the article. Elicit any things that surprise them, e.g. how serious it is, what it is, boys and girls participate, etc.
4 **Key:** 1 C  2 B  3 D  4 A
5 **Key:** A pom poms  B whistle  C ribbons  D team  E audience  F make-up
6 Students can read again to answer questions.
   **Key:** 1 F  2 T  3 T  4 F  5 F  6 F
7 Students discuss the questions in pairs and then feedback.
8 Students match.
   **Key:** chant – a short rhythmic poem  clap – put your hands together  tough – strong  stomp – put your foot on the ground loudly  beat – be the winner  yell – shout very loudly  slap – hit
9 Go through both chants with the class. Model the pronunciation and intonation. Ask students to mark the stressed words. Divide the class into two groups and give each group a different chant. The students practise reciting the chants enthusiastically. Choose one student to be the director/conductor of each group. The students perform the

chants. If possible, record them.

10 In pairs the students find a name for a team and write their own chant. If successful students should recite their chants.

## 29 A SONG FOR EUROPE?

1 Lead in by asking students to discuss the questions first in pairs and then in the full group.

2 The students do the quiz together. They should not leave blanks but guess answers when they don't know.
   **Key:** 1 1956  2 French  3 France  4 Abba  5 Swedish
   6 Honey Pie  7 May  8 over 40  9 more than 100 million
   10 Ireland
   Elicit any other Eurovision facts that the students know, e.g. names of any songs from their countries or others, etc.

3 Students read to answer the question.
   **Key:** positive

4 Students label the picture.
   **Key:** A stage  B solo artist  C duo  D glam rock  E audience
   F drum  G clapping  H cheering

5 Elicit the idea of formality from the students by asking how many ways they can say hello, who they would use these expressions with and in what situations. Then ask what we can say to someone who has done well. Students look at the questions and make their choices.
   **Key:** 1 1 C  2 A  3 B  2 1 B  2 A  3 C

6 Students work on an imaginary song for Europe in pairs. First elicit some useful lexis, for example:  type of song – ballad, glam, rock, pop, love song, folk, traditional   singers – solo artist, duo, boy band, girl band   clothes – sexy, formal, casual, outrageous

7 Students present their song to the group. List the choices on the board. The students then discuss and make their choices in pairs and give their vote to the class.

8 Students write the report in class or at home.

## 30 SCENT-SITIVE?

1 Ask students to name the senses and then refer them to the questions which they discuss in pairs. Feedback.

2 Students do the quiz together.
   **Key:** 1 taste is 75% smell. The brain interprets signals from nose and tongue to make up a taste.  2 b 1 million in each nostril. Each cell is much bigger than ours.  3 True  4a We can detect differences between four and ten thousand if we are young and healthy. 5a There are 7 different types of smell.

3 Elicit different types of advertising, e.g. TV/radio/magazines, etc. You may need to pre-teach some lexis, e.g. experiment/packaging, etc.  Students read both leaflets and answer the questions.
   **Key:** 1 A  2 A  3 A  4 A  5 B  6 B

4 **Key:** 1 about  2 having  3 grateful  4 hope  5 of  6 past
   7 through

5 **Key:** A garlic  B lemon  C sausages  D cleaning products
   E packaging  F shelf

6 Students fill in the questionnaire individually then check and discuss their answers in pairs. Feedback to the full group.

7 Students work in pairs or small groups to think of different smells for the different shops, e.g. travel agent – sea smells for cruises/coconuts for beaches  sports shop – fresh orange juice  clothes – cocktails for party clothes  jewellery shop – expensive perfume  book shop – fresh print.  Alternatively they could think of smells the shops shouldn't have, e.g. sweat in a sports shop/smoke in a clothes shop, etc.

8 The students write the e-mail in class or at home.

## TEST 3 READING

1 C  2 B  3 C  4 B  5 B  6 C  7 A  8 E  9 B  10 D  11 F  12 F
13 T  14 F  15 T  16 T  17 F  18 F  19 T  20 F  21 A  22 C
23 A  24 C  25 B

## 31 FUNHOUSE

1 Lead in by asking students about their ideal houses and what

---

they think a very modern house will have in it. Students then talk about the questions in pairs and feedback to the group.
   **Key:** 1 C

2 Students look at the picture and read the list to find the things shown.
   **Key:** 1 3  2 4  3 9  4 10

3 Students listen to tick the items.
   **Key:** 3, 4, 7, 8, 9
   Check the meanings of the other items.

4 **Key:** C

5 Students listen and choose the correct answers. Ask students if they would like to live in this house. Why/not?
   **Key:** 1 C  2 B  3 C  4 A  5 B

**Tapescript**
*Abby: Hi! I got an amazing e-mail from my English penfriend today. You will never guess what she's doing.*
*Brian: Go on then. Tell me.*
*Abby: It's incredible. Her dad works for an electronics company and the whole family is taking part in this experiment. They're going to spend six months in a house which is completely hi-tech!*
*Brian: What do you mean – "hi-tech"?*
*Abby: Well, it's like – it's a sort of a "house of the future"!*
*Brian: Wow!*
*Abby: Yeah! Can you imagine?! Maggie, her brother Benjy and her mum and dad have this crazy house to play in for six months!*
*Brian: So, are they in there now?*
*Abby: Yeah. They went in yesterday and Maggie e-mailed me this morning. They've got glass floors – so it's really light, but a bit weird, and the windows clean themselves!*
*Brian: I don't follow you.*
*Abby: There's something on the windows that means you don't ever have to clean them.*
*Brian: You're kidding.*
*Abby: Nope. You can change the pictures on the walls electronically to suit your mood.*
*Brian: Sorry – you've lost me.*
*Abby: You can access pictures from your computer and show them on your walls. It means that you can have different pictures so that you don't get bored!*
*Brian: Cool!*
*Abby: There's also a waterproof screen in the bathroom so you can watch TV and DVDs.*
*Brian: Waterproof?*
*Abby: So water can't get into it and electrocute you!*
*Brian: That's a relief!*
*Abby: And there's intercom from room to room – and video if you want it.*
*Brian: Why intercom?*
*Abby: So they can talk to each other from any room in the house! And the phones talk to you – they tell you the name of the caller.*
*Brian: Like – " Your father is calling you!"*
*Abby: Yeah. Everything talks! The cooker, the weather monitor….*
*Brian: Weather what?*
*Abby: In the morning a gadget tells you what the weather's like outside before you get up!*
*Brian: Weird! I think I could live like that for a while but not for too long. It would do my head in!*

6 **Key:** 1 C  2 D  3 E  4 F  5 B  6 A
   Students give each other a situation for them to respond to. Give an example, e.g. It's only going to cost 20 euros to repair the window! Feedback situations to the full group.

7 Students listen again to note down how Abby explains the words.
   **Key:** hi–tech – it's a sort of house of the future; Waterproof – water can't get in; Weather monitor – it tells you what the weather's like.
   Give students some more words to explain. They can be words the students have recently learned, e.g. diet – it's when you want to get slimmer and you don't eat much.

8 Students work in pairs to invent gadgets and draw or write about them in the picture.

9 Go through Brian's expressions with some more examples.

Students swap partners and show them their pictures. They ask and answer questions about the new gadgets.
10 Students write the paragraph in class or at home.

## 32 SHOPPING PLANS

1 Lead in by asking students if they like going shopping. Why/not? Divide students into groups. They use the survey questions with the others in their group. Feedback.

2 Students work together to find the words.
**Key:** casual outdoor sports work summer smart party formal underwear kids night foot
Check meanings and ask for an example of each type of clothing.

3 **Key:** 1 D 2 E 3 B 4 A 5 C
Elicit other words connected with a shop. "Where do they hang the new clothes?" (rack) "In changing rooms what are the individual small rooms called?" (cubicles) "What do we call changing rooms for both sexes (unisex)?"

4 Students listen and tick the clothing items.
**Key:** casual outdoor sports smart party underwear foot kids night

**Tapescript**

*Manager: OK – thanks for coming everyone. This meeting is to tell you all about the changes we are going to make to the layout of the shop. As you know – sales are down. One reason is the competition from the big clothing stores. So we have to make some changes to get the customers in here – and not only the girls. We want the guys to come in as well. So here's the new layout.*
*The customer comes through the door and the first thing he or she sees, immediately in front of him or her is our new range of designer accessories. Belts in the centre, bags on the right, hats and scarves on the left. The customer turns right and there's flashy jewellery and make up. This is the girly direction. Men turn left and there's male body products. Girls continue round and on the right there's underwear and then night wear. On their left there are three main racks. The first is party wear. Next to that is smart wear – suits, blouses and then there's casual wear. That includes sports items and jeans. The same on the guys' side. The first rack on the right for them is cool stuff for partying, then smart business/work clothes and finally casual wear. On their left they've got men's underwear, socks, etc., then outdoor stuff – coats, jackets. Following on from the racks at the other end of the shop we have footwear, shoes and boots – men's on the left, women's on the right. Behind that the whole of the back section is changing rooms – unisex or split – we're still thinking about that. And of course, bang in the centre we have the most important place in the shop – the cash desk!! In front of that – behind the accessories there'll be a kids section – so, with luck, there'll be something for everyone, we'll be packed out, make millions and everyone will have a salary increase! OK? Any questions?*

5 Students answer the two questions from memory.
**Key:** 1 sales are down 2 both

6 Revise easy directions and position words. Write some examples on the board, e.g. "Turn left/right" "in front of/behind", etc. Students listen again to complete the sections.
**Key:** Bags – F Hats and scarves – E Jewellery – A
Male body products – C Girls' underwear – B
Girls' partywear – G Girl's casual wear – J
Men's outdoorwear – D Men's partywear – H
Men's smartwear – I Men's footwear – L
Changing rooms – M Cash desk – K

7 Check that students understand the meanings of the items before doing the task.
**Key:** 1 footwear 2 nightwear 3 nightwear 4 casualwear 5 partywear 6 jewellery 7 male body products 8 kidswear 9 accessories
Ask students what items they last bought from these sections.

8 Set up the discussion task and elicit/revise useful expressions for opinion asking and giving, e.g. "What do you think about …?" "Music would be a good idea because …". Put them on the board.

9 Look at the expressions for position with the students. Refer them back to their shop plan and practise by asking questions, e.g. "Where is the cash desk?" Instruct students to plan a new shop lay out on a piece of paper. They then tell each other where things are in the new shop and they

complete a new floor plan.
10 Students write about their shop in class or at home. This can be a straightforward description or a short advertisement starting "Come to the opening of the new …"

## 33 MUSIC MUSIC

1 Lead in by asking students about their favourite music and whether they've been to many live concerts. Elicit the word "festival". Students discuss questions in pairs and feedback.

2 Students match the synonyms.
**Key:** views – 3 gig – 4 outfits – 6 line up – 5
the season – 1 spectacular – 2

3 Students predict what they think will be mentioned.

4 Students listen to check.
**Key:** dates, places, stars, contact numbers

**Tapescript**

*Hi there! This is Sandy Donaldson bringing you all the music news and views on Southern Summertime Radio. So, music lovers, these sunny days and high temperatures mean only one thing – the festival season is coming! The big news at the moment is that Britney is touring this summer and she's playing at Bristol, Oxford and Exeter open-air festivals. She will finish here at our very own gig in Hyde Park. This will be a spectacular tour. She's spending a fortune on outfits and effects – so go see the little lady herself while you have the opportunity. Elton John is playing the Plymouth Park Festival in July, which is great news for all those fans who missed him this time last year. And the really big news is that we can now tell you the line up for the Forest Festival just outside Southampton in August. Fingers on those phones boys and girls because you will NOT want to miss this event! If I say Coldplay, The Coral, Snow Patrol, Keane – does that make your hearts beat faster? Well, it's true – all those bands and more are in the Forest line up. The weather forecast is good for August so the ground will be hard and dry for all your tents! Tickets are going on sale at 9.30 this morning and I can tell you – there won't be any left by this evening. So, get dialling and reserve your space at THE place for the summer! 05705499976*

5 1 festival 2 big 3 touring 4 playing 5 a fortune on outfits 6 forecast 7 dialling

6 Students listen again to complete the information. Ask them to record this on a separate piece of paper.
**Key:** Britney – Bristol, Oxford, Exeter, summer; Elton John – Plymouth, July; Cold Play, The Coral, Snow Patrol, Keane – Southampton, August

7 Students ask questions about the table, e.g. Plymouth – "Who's playing at Plymouth?" "When's he's playing there?" etc.

8 Set the situation by eliciting information about an imaginary festival. When/how many days/who's playing/where it is, etc. Put this on the board. In pairs, students make arrangements for going to the festival and write down the information.

9 Students change partners and role play the phone conversation – making funny noises at important points so that their partner has to ask "Where are we meeting?", etc. Remind students that present continuous is used for arrangements that have already been made. Feedback.

10 Students write the e-mail in class or at home.

## 34 THE BALLAD OF JEN AND STANLEY

1 Lead in by putting some of the expressions on the board and asking students what they're used to describe. Elicit/tell students that they are also used to describe people. Students look at the adjectives and write them in the correct column. Feedback. Ask students to guess meanings and then clarify.
**Key:** positive – wicked, classy, superstar, diamond, amazing, cool, sassy negative – loser, dull, plastic, freaky, weirdo, doughnut, fake, boring, cringey, creepy
wicked, cool – great; classy – has style; superstar, diamond – helpful, friendly; sassy – knows what he/she wants; plastic – false (to look at); freaky, weirdo – strange; doughnut – silly; cringey – embarrassing; creepy – yuk.

2 **Key:** dull loser fake creepy cool diamond sassy superstar wicked plastic amazing classy

3 Tell students that they are going to listen to a ballad (a story poem) about mountain bikes and cars. Ask them to first

discuss the advantages and disadvantages of both. Feedback.

4 Students listen to identify adjectives.

Key: wicked, classy, superstar, diamond, amazing, cool, sassy, loser, dull, doughnut, creepy

**Tapescript**

*Once upon a time there was*
*A wicked guy, but sad – because*
*His sassy girlfriend didn't like*
*Him riding on his mountain bike.*
*She thought, "It's dull to spend the day*
*Riding bikes so far away!*
*It really isn't worth the bother."*
*And Stan, her man, tried hard to stop her*
*Leaving him for diamond Matt*
*Who had the most amazing hat!*
*Matt drove a car, a cool Ferrari*
*And Jenna's eyes went wide and starry*
*To see him stand so strong and manly*
*So different from her poor old Stanley.*
*One day, however, cold and wet*
*Ferrari stopped. Our Jen, upset*
*Needed to catch a train at ten*
*But the car refused to start again.*
*Jen phoned dear Stan, "What can I do?"*
*"Sit tight," he said, "I'll be there soon."*
*Our superstar did what he said,*
*Threw back the sheets – jumped out of bed.*
*Creepy Matt was sitting, phoning*
*A break-down truck, and Jen was moaning*
*"Get me out – I'll miss my train*
*I'll never drive with you again!*
*You silly doughnut, my classy Stan*
*Is strong and cool, a RE-AL man!*
*He'd never let me down like this*
*I hate the day we ever kissed!"*
*Then up comes Stan, two bikes in hand*
*Jen climbs on one, life is so grand!*
*The bikes climb up the icy hill*
*While loser Matt must pay the bill*
*For towing him back to his home*
*Ferrari man, now all alone.*
*While Stan and Jen together see*
*That mountain bikes can make you free.*

5 Students put pictures in order and listen again to check.

Key: F, B, I, E, J, A, D, C, G, H

6 Students complete the rhyming words then listen again.

Key: 1 because 2 bike 3 away 4 stop her 5 hat 6 starry 7 Stanley 8 upset 9 again 10 soon 11 bed 12 moaning 13 again 14 man 15 kissed 16 grand 17 bill 18 alone 19 free

Check meanings of new words and put in different contexts. Note that the more common pronunciation of 'again' rhymes with 'ten'.

7 Students find rhyming words. Feedback, writing up examples, e.g. hand, star, free, pear, ring, toy, fun, fat, high, play, wine, stone. Point out that spelling and sound can be very different!

8 Students write their ballads together. They read them to the rest of the group.

## 35 PARTY TIME

1 Lead in by asking students if they go to a lot of parties and what sort of parties they had when they were younger. Students discuss questions in pairs and feedback to group.

2 Key: 1 up 2 on 3 on 4 about 5 at 6 in 7 for 8 over

Check meanings and give other examples to practise, e.g. I like tennis but I'm not very good … it.

3 Elicit the meaning of "sleepover". Students read through the questions first and then listen to do the task.

Key: 1 M 2 D 3 M 4 D 5 D 6 M 7 B 8 D 9 M 10 B

**Tapescript**

*Presenter: Good morning everyone out there and a big "hello" to our guests today – David Fellows and Mary Purcell. You probably know David's name as*

*he has been in the news recently – when he returned from holiday and found…. Well, I'll let David tell you himself. Mary is a mother with her own story to tell. Let's go first to David. So, David, tell us – why have you been in our newspapers this week?*

*David: Hi! Well – I certainly didn't want to be in the papers. Janet, my wife, and I went to Spain with our younger son for a short holiday and we left our older son, Mark, at home – he was studying for his exams. Mark's sixteen. He asked us if it would be OK to have a friend or two to stay while we were away and we said "Fine, but not too many!"*

*Mary: First big mistake!*

*David: You are so right. But we were feeling guilty about leaving him behind and he's a good kid. Anyway, we got back to find that our lovely house was a complete disaster area. He'd invited six friends over – too many I know – but in fact 100 kids arrived. There were fights, they smashed the furniture, computers, pictures… It cost us over £15,000 to repair.*

*Mary: Wow! That's serious money. Why were there so many gatecrashers?*

*David: Apparently, the word went round Mark's school – a very good and expensive private school – that he was having an "empty" as they say these days – and they decided it was party time. Poor Mark didn't know what to do. What about you Mary – did the whole town come round for a party while you were away too?*

*Mary: Goodness no. Nothing like that. My daughter, Holly, is much younger than your son – she's only ten. But her age group are into sleepovers and she's been trying to persuade us that we should let her invite a few friends over for her birthday instead of the usual teen party. It's the guilt thing again. She's very good at that. "Everybody else has sleepovers on their birthdays!" "I won't have any friends if I can't have a sleepover." "I'm so lonely without any brothers or sisters." They keep on and it's difficult to say "no" after a while so we said "OK. You can invite two friends." She invited six. They all slept in her bedroom on the floor. They watched videos all night. They were jumping, shouting, arguing, fighting. Goodness knows what they were eating – they were sick all over the place. My husband and I got no sleep at all and we had to take one child home at three o'clock in the morning because she had stomachache. What a nightmare. So, I understand a little about what you experienced David. Will you ever let your son have a party while you're away again?*

*David: You must be joking. His next party will be at his own house and I will not be paying for it. And you? Any more sleepovers?*

*Mary: No way! And learning from your experience – she won't be having any "empties" when she's older either!*

*Presenter: But that's a bit hard on the kids, isn't it?*

*David: Have you got any children?*

*Presenter: Er, no*

*Mary: Then we'll have this conversation again when you do!!*

4 Students listen again to complete the answers.

Key: 1 Mark 2 Holly 3 furniture/computers/pictures 4 she had stomachache 5 the noise 6 one 7 two 8 none

5 Students talk about different party types. Feedback and put ideas on board, e.g beach parties, formal prom parties, barbeques, pool parties, theme parties, kids parties, etc. – the more different or extreme the better.

6 Put the eight pieces of information for the invitation on the board. Students take a piece of paper and write "Please come to my …… party" at the top. The students fold over this line and pass the paper on. The next student writes "On ……" etc. The students should write the information without knowing what the previous student has written. Encourage them to be creative so that the final reading is funny.

7 Go through the expressions used in turn taking and encourage students to use them when they have short conversations with other students. They can practise them by talking about a party they both went to. Feedback.

8 Students write their account in class or at home.

## 36 I'M SEEING THINGS

1 Lead in by referring to the title and asking students if they have ever "seen things". Students complete the crosswords.

Key: A: 1 ghost 2 death 3 butler 4 stains 5 Scotland 6 stabbed 7 murder B: 1 courtyard 2 hall 3 staircase 4 kitchen 5 ballroom 6 bedroom

**Mystery word:** haunted castle.

Check any unfamiliar words

**2** Elicit what a tour guide recording is. Students listen to the recording. Ask if they think it is real or a "spoof".
**Key:** It could be real – if the ghosts are models.
Ask how they think the tourists feel. Students will probably need to listen again to find the word not used.
**Key:** ghost

**Tapescript**

*Welcome to Carver Castle – the most haunted building in Scotland. There have been many deaths here. This is a tour guide recording for the Scottish Tourist Board and my name is…Vincent. So, let us begin. You are standing at the main entrance to Carver Castle, in front of the great wooden doors. The doors open. Welcome. The butler who greets you is Jarvis. He died 200 years ago from old age – he was 99 – but he still likes to welcome visitors. Step into the entrance hall. Look at the floor. The bloodstains there are from a double murder in 1795. A thief stabbed the Lord and Lady of the house in this hall when they caught him inside the castle. No one can clean the blood. Look up and you can see the grand staircase. On the bottom stair is Grandmother Frances. Her eldest son, Alexander, pushed her down the stairs in 1809. He wanted her money. Step over her and climb the stairs. There at the bend is young Martha Dooley. See how she hides her face. She cannot stop crying for her lost love – the young Duke of Westchester, killed at Waterloo. Come up to the first floor and walk along the corridor. You can hear laughter here. That is mad Agnes, locked in her room for 50 years. And if you go into the third room on the left you can feel the heat of the fire that destroyed the bedroom when the first Lord Carver found his beautiful wife Elizabeth in bed with his brother, George. Can you smell the burning sheets?*

*Return downstairs and enter the old kitchen. You will hear the hissing of boiling water. I shall not tell you what is cooking in the giant pan on the cooker. You do not want to know. And can you feel the cold coming from the open door? On a freezing night in December when there was deep snow on the ground, a poor traveller asked for shelter. They refused him and he died out there in the courtyard, in the snow. Now, turn back and follow the music to the great ballroom. There at the end a man is standing. He is playing the violin. He has no head. The third Lord Carver cut off his head because he played the wrong music for the Lord's lovely wife.*

*And now, it is time to return to the outside world. Go back to the wooden doors. Oh dear, the doors have closed. Turn the handle. [sounds of handle turning] Locked? Try the key? It will not turn? Well, it's going to be a looooong night!*

**3 Key:** (examples)1 bloodstains  2 laughter  3 burning  4 cold air
**4 Key:** Martha Dooley - on the stairs;  Jarvis - entrance; Grandmother Frances - bottom of the stairs; Elizabeth & George - 3rd bedroom; the traveller - courtyard; the violonist - ballroom; Agnes - corridor; Lord & Lady Carver - hall
**5** Students complete the table together.
**Key:** 1 Jarvis: old age, old  2 Lord and Lady Carver: stabbed, caught a thief  3 Grandmother Frances: fell down stairs, son wanted her money  4 Elizabeth and George: burned to death, husband found them  5 The traveller: froze to death, no one gave him shelter  6 The violinist: head cut off, played the wrong music
**6** Students work in pairs to invent some new ghosts for the castle with their stories. Swap partners and give a new short tour guide. Other student adds to the plan.
**7** Students write the article in class or at home. Start: "Among the ghosts that people have seen in the castle are …"

## 37  MY BIG FOOT

**1** Lead in by eliciting meaning of "embarrassed". Give a situation e.g. "Yesterday I ……. . I was SO ….." Students find words from the main word.
**Key:** (examples) bar  dress  sad  made  mad  same  mess etc.
**2 Key:** 1 red  2 think  3 cringe  4 foot
**3** Give an example and then students talk together. Feedback.
**4** Ask students how you can "put your foot in it" on the phone. Play the conversations twice. Students answer the questions.

**Tapescript**

*Conversation A*
*Connie: Oh – that's Stu. He said he'd phone at 6.*
*Kathy: Well, answer it then.*
*Connie: I can't – I'm painting my nails! Could you answer it Kath?*

*Kathy: No probs. Hiya.*
*Nasal voice: Oh hello! Can I speak to Connie please?*
*Kathy: [putting on a nasal voice too] Well, I'll have to think about that.*
*Voice: I beg your pardon?*
*Kathy: Well, she's too busy to speak to you at the moment. She's doing some painting – pictures on the kitchen wall actually.*
*Voice: She's doing what?*
*Kathy: And after that she's going to an all night party in London with the boy next door!*
*Voice: I'm sorry. Who are you?*
*Kathy: Oh for goodness sake Stu – take your fingers off your nose and speak properly.*
*Voice: My name is not Stu. I'm Connie's father. Now can I speak to my daughter please?*
*Kathy: Oh …*

*Conversation B*
*Sexy voice: Hello. 07804399427*
*Jake: Hi sexy!*
*Sexy voice: I'm sorry?*
*Jake: No, I'm really sorry. I haven't phoned before because I couldn't find the number.*
*Sexy voice: Yes?*
*Jake: You see – I wrote it on the back of the menu and well – I mixed it up with some papers and gave it in with my last English essay.*
*Sexy voice: That's not a bad excuse!*
*Jake: Thanks. I got the essay – and the menu – back today. And I thought, maybe – do you fancy coming out with me tonight?*
*Sexy voice: And you are?*
*Jake: Me? I'm Jake. Don't you remember? I was sitting at the table next to you in Luigi's restaurant last Friday. You gave me your number? I've got short, dark hair, blue eyes and I…*
*Sexy voice: Right Jake. I'm sure I would remember you but unfortunately I wasn't at Luigi's last Friday.*
*Jake: Oh blast! I've got the wrong number.*
*Sexy voice: No – you've got the right number. I wasn't at Luigi's but my daughter was.*

**Key:** A 1 Kathy  2 her friend is busy (painting her nails) 3 Connie  4 Kathy thinks it's her friend's boyfriend – Stu but it's her father.  5 Connie's dad has a funny voice and Kathy tells him to talk properly!
B  1 Jake  2 a girl from a restaurant  3 to make a date  4 the voice says she wasn't at the restaurant  5 the girl's mum.
**5** Ask students for their ideas. Play the next part.
**Key:** Kathy B  Jake A

**Tapescript**

*Conversation A*
*Kathy: I am SO sorry. I thought you were Stu, Connie's boyfriend.*
*Voice: Stu Taylor? She's not seeing that terrible boy is she? I don't believe that she can …*
*Kathy: Connie! It's your father and I think I've really put my foot in it!*
*Conversation B*
*Jake: Ah … er … (hangs up)*

**6** Go through the expressions used in an embarrassing situation. Students should be careful about intonation and emphasis.
**7** Set up the role play. Go through the different situations so that students are clear about the mistaken identity theme. Students do the role plays. Feedback.
**8** Students write the e-mail in class or at home.

## 38  LOVE IT OR HATE IT?

**1** Lead in by asking students to sing or hum as many ringtones as they can. In small groups they ask each other the questions on the survey. Feedback and collate results on the board.
**2 Key:** Positive – catchy, wicked, brill
Negative – irritating, moronic, demented
Either – electronic, different, repetitive, new
Check unfamiliar words. Ask students if they can give an example of these!
**3 Key:** A 4  B 1  C 3  D 2
**4** Ask students if they have heard of "crazy frog" and can they sing/hum the tune. Students listen to answer the question.

**Key:** It's the first number 1 from a ringtone.
**Tapescript**

*Presenter: Love it or hate it, the first number one CD in the UK from a ringtone will certainly not be the last. Crazy Frog jumped to number one in front of Coldplay and everyone is talking about it. So, we are too! We have a call from Sadie Jones. Hi Sadie – your opinion on the Crazy Frog please!*
*Sadie: Crazy frog is brill! It's catchy, it's different – you can download it onto your phone and it drives the parents nuts! It's real pop music. Pop music is for us kids – it's not something your mum and dad listen to! They've got Elvis and The Beatles and Status Quo. And Crazy frog – well it's so new – everyone's singing it! Wicked, wicked!*
*Presenter: I think we know how Sadie feels! And on line 3 we have Maria. Do you agree with Sadie? Is the Crazy Frog the best music ever?!*
*Maria: You are joking? I cannot believe that song – can you call it a song? It's number 1 in the UK charts! I'm sorry, but that is not music. It's a ringtone for goodness sake! It's electronic, it's repetitive, it's so irritating I want to scream everytime I hear it on TV. And at the moment it's everywhere on TV. You can't escape it. It's moronic. What is happening to the music world? A band like Coldplay with a superb song are at number 2 while a frog on a motorbike is number 1? Puh leese! It's not even a green frog – it's blue – it walks on two legs – it has a tummy button! It's not just crazy – it's demented!*
*Presenter: Well, pretty strong opinions there! In the studio we have expert Ted Bowls to comment on this new trend. Ted, is this the end of music as we know it?*
*Ted: Or the beginning? I know – Crazy Frog is very irritating for anyone over 18 – although it is popular with university students and younger workers. I think they see it as a craze and a symbol of being young. Really, I don't understand the problem. No – it's not the end of music. Elvis wasn't the end of music, nor were Queen although our parents thought they were! Is the strange "ding – dinging" of the frog that different from the "wop lop a loo bop" or "ba – be – de – de – ba" of the 1950s and 60s? Your first caller was right. It's new, it's different and kids love it. That's what pop music is about. Kids love to love what their parents hate! That will never change! Good luck to the frog – but don't allow him anywhere near me!*

**5** Students listen again.
 **Key:** 1 S  2 T  3 S  4 S  5 M  6 T  7 M, T
**6 Key:** 1 B  2 A  3 B
**7** Look through the expressions in the speech bubble. Students practise by repeating with stress on important words, e.g. scream/awful, etc. Give an example of something about your parents/older generation that drives you nuts. Students discuss the questions in pairs, using expressions. Feedback.
**8** Elicit some differences between what parents and children like/dislike. Write on the board. Look at the model sentence. Students write some more sentences using contrastive links.

## 39 DREAM JOB

**1** Lead in by asking what jobs you can have working for a magazine. List suggestions on the board. Students match the drawings with the jobs and then label them.
 **Key:** 1 G photographer  2 D doctor  3 C tester  4 B reviewer  5 E model  6 A journalist  7 F designer
**2** Students discuss the questions in pairs and feedback.
**3** Before listening students match the synonyms.
 **Key:** 1 C  2 E  3 D  4 B  5 A
 Practise new lexis by asking questions using the words, e.g. "Is there a downside to living in this area? What can be a pain when you're trying to study? What stuff do you take on holiday with you?" etc.
**4** Students read the cards so they know what information they're listening for. Play each section twice and give time to complete the card before moving on.
 **Key:**

| Name | Greta | Hope | James |
|---|---|---|---|
| Magazine | Great Gear | – | Best Car |
| Job | Model | road tester | Journalist |
| Good points | money, travel | keep stuff, variety, meeting people | interviews drivers, drive cars, money, travel, he decides what to do |
| Bad points | long days, diets, early nights | stress, odd people | no regular work |

**Tapescript**

*GRETA: Hiya! I'm Greta and I work for Great Gear magazine. I'm a model. It's a great job but it can be very hard. The days are long, I'm always on a diet and I have to go to bed really early. But the money's good and I get to model some fantastic clothes in some brill places. Last week I was in California modelling swimwear with some cool surfer dudes! It was so hot! But then, next week I'm in Scotland, up a mountain to model ski clothes! Brr! I started modelling when I was sixteen. I won a magazine competition and the prize was a modelling job. I was July's covergirl! I was SO excited! And that was it. I've never been out of work. But a model doesn't have a long career – so I have to work as hard as I can now while I'm young. When I'm older, maybe I'll become a journalist. Who knows? But I love the magazine world.*
*HOPE: My name's Hope and I'm a road-tester. No, that doesn't mean I drive cars all day! I try new things and see what they're like – like make up or celebrity keep fit videos and stuff. I also try on a lot of clothes and test the sizes and materials. It's cool. I get to keep some of the stuff I test and my days are always different. One day I'm testing perfume and the next I'm cooking a recipe to see if it works! I meet loads of cool people in my job and I love working for a magazine. There's a great buzz about getting the next edition out on time. If there's a downside, it's probably the stress. Also, some of the people in the business are a bit "precious" but there again, there are people like that everywhere!*
*JAMES: Hi. I'm James. I'm a journalist and I usually write for "Best Car" magazine which is brill because I'm a car fanatic! I've always wanted to be a journalist. I started writing when I was about ten and I've never stopped. I really love my job. I get to interview racing drivers and car manufacturers and I write articles on new cars, races, safety, etc. I even get to drive them sometimes! I'm free lance so it means I don't have regular work. That can be a pain but there again, I'm free to write for who I like, when I like! If I want to go off on holiday tomorrow – I can! The money is very good and I'm always travelling, especially when there are big international racing meetings. I wouldn't change my job for the world!*

**5 Key:** 1 H  2 J  3 H  4 G  5 G  6 G  7 J
**6** Elicit meaning of *I get to* … from examples. (I'm allowed to … I can do something I'm not usually allowed to do) Students make examples of their own. Feedback to board.
**7** Students do the task without looking at their partner's text. Give an example "What's the name of the person?"
 **Key:** Wendy Masters  magazine  26  "Bananas"  9 p.m.  4 a.m.  watches TV  hot drink  12.30  jam  bacon  two cups of coffee  gym  Lindsay  an hour  Mark  "Maples"  Canadian  red  magazine
**8** Students write notes for a mini presentation of another magazine job and give it to the class. Students should think about what you do in the job, what the good and bad points are, the routine, the sort of person, e.g. start: The job of a photographer is very interesting. A photographer is artistic …

## 40 PAYBACK TIME?

**1** Lead in by putting the word "Questionnaire" on the board and eliciting where you can find them. Students discuss questions. Feedback.
**2** Elicit the sort of questions that might be asked.
 **Key:** about your habits, your likes and dislikes, what you would do in different situations, etc.
**3** Students listen and identify which quizzes are mentioned.
 **Key:** 1, 3, 4, 6
 Focus on the last one and clarify meaning of revenge = forgive and forget.

**Tapescript**
*You have reached the personality quiz phone line. Choose from one of these options. For Best Mates, press 1. For Making Money, press 2. For Hearts and flowers, press 3. For Forgive and forget, press 4.*

**4 Key:** 1 e R  2 f R  3 a F  4 b F  5 c R  6 d F
 Put the items into context for the students, e.g. "He argued with his girlfriend but they've made up now." to indicate how strong or weak the expressions are.
**5** Go through the items and elicit meaning before the students do the task.
 **Key:** 1 immature  2 argument  3 go jump  4 dump  5 sensible  6 nasty

**6** Let students read through the gapped text. Play the recording and students listen to fill the gaps. Play again. Students check with their partners. Explain any unfamiliar lexis.
Key: see tapescript

**Tapescript**
*1 After an argument how long have you been angry with someone?*
*A a few hours   B a few days   C a few weeks   D for ever*
*2 Someone tells you that your boyfriend or girlfriend is going out with someone else in secret. What do you do?*
*A talk to him/her   B dump him/her   C cut up his/her clothes   D shout at him/her*
*3 You plan a night out with your friends. No one comes. What do you do?*
*A never speak to your friends again   B have a big argument   C think "Oh well" and ask them out again.   D get angry but forget it tomorrow.*
*4 A friend makes a joke about you. What do you do?*
*A laugh with everyone   B talk to your friend later   C shout at him/her in front of everyone   D never speak to him/her again.*
*5 You meet your ex with his/her new partner. What do you do?*
*A leave   B say hello   C give them a dirty look   D argue*
*6 Your ex breaks up with his/her new partner. Do you …*
*A feel sorry for him/her?   B feel pleased?   C tell all your friends?   D phone him/her to laugh about it*
*7 Your ex wants to go out with you again. What do you do?*
*A kiss and make up   B make up but be careful   C tell him/her to go jump   D take some time to think about it.*
*8 You go out with someone new. Do you …*
*A tell the new person everything about your ex?   B explain why you broke up?   C keep talking about your ex?   D never talk about your ex?*

**7** Students complete the questionnaire individually and exchange with their partners who calculate their scores.

**8** Play the analysis and students match words to the sections. Discuss the analyses with the students. They must match the score range to the sections.
Key: 1 B   2 D   3 A   4 C   5 B   6 A   7 D   8 C

**Tapescript**
*28–32 It is nearly impossible for you to forgive people who hurt you. This is bad for your future relationships. You can be immature and plan nasty paybacks. Grow up! You must learn to be more forgiving or you will never have a long relationship.*
*20–27 You often don't want arguments to finish and it can be difficult for people to get close to you. You like to get your revenge but unfortunately you don't often succeed! Try to talk to people about how you feel, not complain behind their backs.*
*10–19 You don't usually hold a grudge but you can be hard when it's necessary. You are mature and sensible and you are good in different situations. If things go wrong you can always start again.*
*Less than 10 You are very forgiving but sometimes too nice. You have a soft centre but be careful. Not everyone is as nice as you are and you can get hurt quite easily.*

**9** Students speculate on what might have happened to provoke these paybacks.

**10** Students write a short questionnaire together. Give them a model question/situation with three possible answers. Students swap partners and use their questionnaires.

## VOCABULARY 2

**1** 1 C   2 B   3 B   4 A   5 C
**2** 1 I worked my socks off at the supermarket.
2 English grammar really does my head in.
3 You have to put the past behind you.
4 I am always putting my foot in it.
5 She hurt him but he'll get his own back.
**3** 1 for   2 up   3 back   4 over   5 up   6 past   7 away   8 out   9 at   10 on
**4** 1 stuff   2 pain   3 downside   4 buzz   5 outfit   6 gig   7 changing   8 revenge   9 buds   10 reputation
**5** 1 versatile   2 addictive   3 outspoken   4 catchy   5 competitive   6 gross   7 controversial   8 time consuming   9 rewarding   10 imaginative
**6** 1 clap   2 chant   3 yell   4 cheer   5 refund   6 dump   7 cringe   8 explode
**7** Across: 1 recipe   5 fit   6 embarrassed   9 shy   11 burns

12 waterproof;   Down: 2 covergirl   3 weirdo   4 gatecrasher   7 bling   8 sensible   10 shift

## TEST 4 LISTENING
*Play each part twice.*
1 B   2 C   3 C   4 C   5 A   6 A   7 B   8 C   9 B   10 A   11 A
12 B   13 stuff   14 Saturday 6th June   15 footwear
16 coffee bar   17 special play area   18 20%   19 wine
20 3pm   21 shopping mall   22 F   23 T   24 F   25 F   26 F   27 T

**Tapescript**
*Part 1*
*1 If you look at the new layout you can see that the partywear is in front of the cash desk. It's behind the casual wear. It's in a good position.*
*2 A: Have you heard the line up for the Valley festival?*
*   B: No. Who's playing?*
*   A: Coldplay can't come. But Oasis and Green Day are both playing on the Saturday!*
*3 A: I met Jay's sister yesterday.*
*   B: What's she like?*
*   A: Oh – she's a bit of a doughnut!*
*4 I went to Mike's party on Friday. It was cool – but there were a few gatecrashers and the house got a bit messed up.*
*5 In 1764 Lord Farchester was the owner of the castle. He was hated by his servants and one of them stabbed him to death in the ballroom.*
*6 I am SO sorry. My mistake. I thought you were my friend's father called George. You're not are you?*
*Part 2*
*This weekend I interviewed David Acorah. Many of you are probably saying "and WHO is David Acorah?" Viewers of the extremely popular TV series "Most Haunted" know him well. He's the UK's top medium. – a person who helps communicate with dead people (and in some cases – pets). David was certainly not what I expected. He started life as a professional footballer for Liverpool. There are some questions about how many games he actually played but there is no question that he was a football player. He's not exactly David Beckham but he doesn't look like the sort of person who sees ghosts either! He's a very nice guy. He's calm and friendly and doesn't get angry when people say nasty things about the show. People have suggested that he's a fake and that everything that happens in his shows is planned. David just smiles. That smile says "people can believe what they want. I know the truth." He tells me a bit about some people in my family who have died and some things about my childhood. He's right. I start to get this weird feeling. Perhaps it's time to go back out into the sunshine and the real world.*
*Part 3*
*We are very proud to announce that our new shop "Designer Stuff" is opening on Saturday 6th June. As the name says we will be selling the latest designer clothes and footwear for both men and women and there will also be a special section for the kids! There will be a coffee bar where you can meet friends and share drinks and cakes and we are planning a special play area for very young children so that you can look through the racks in peace! On the opening day we shall have a special discount of 20% and all customers will get a free glass of wine (not the children of course!). So don't miss the grand opening. 3pm in The Hightown Shopping Mall. Be there!*
*Part 4*
*Sally: Gary. Has Kev talked to you about the party at his place on Saturday?*
*Gary: Yeah. His parents are off on holiday and he's got the house to himself. I think he's invited the whole school!! Should be fun. Are you going?*
*Sally: I might go for an hour or so – but it's going to be packed out and I'm sure there'll be loads of gatecrashers.*
*Gary: The more the merrier!*
*Sally: I don't know. There could be trouble.*
*Gary: You worry too much.*
*Sally: His parents are going to be so angry when they get back.*
*Gary: Well, that's his problem. My parents would never leave me in the house on my own. They know me.*
*Sally: I would be too frightened to have a party with my parents away – think of the mess and broken things!*
*Gary: So, this isn't at your house – it's at Kev's. Now are you coming or not?*
*Sally: Mmmmm.*